NATIVE
AMERICAN

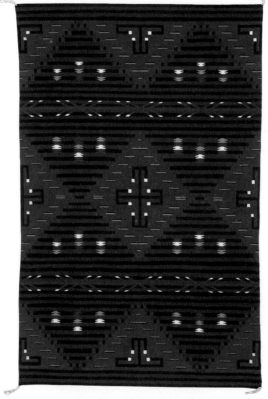

STYLE

NATIVE AMERICAN STYLE

Elmo Baca

M. J. Van Deventer

GIBBS·SMITH
P
PUBLISHER

SALT LAKE CITY

First Edition

02 01 00 99 4 3 2 1

Published by
Gibbs Smith, Publisher
P.O. Box 667
Layton, UT 84041
Orders: (1-800) 748-5439
Visit our web site at www.gibbs-smith.com

Edited by Gail Yngve
Designed by Christine Nasser

Printed and bound in China

Library of Congress Cataloging-in-Publication Data

Baca, Elmo

    Native American style / by Elmo Baca and M. J. Van Deventer.
—1st ed.
      p.   cm.
   ISBN 0-87905-789-0

    1. Indian art—North America. 2. Decorative arts—North America.
3. Indians of North America—Dwellings. 4. Indians of North
America—Religion. I. Van Deventer, M. J. II. Title.
E98.A7B23 1999
970.00497—dc21   97-7802
           CIP

Half Title Page: This Ganado-style Navajo rug won awards at a recent Inter-Tribal Indian Ceremonial in Gallup.

Title Page: Artist C. J. Prophet has adapted ancient Hopi designs from Arizona for his contemporary gourd art.

Dedication Page: Navajo painter Irving Toddy juxtaposes three-dimensional and abstract imagery—traditional and contemporary interfaces of a mother and daughter in *Ancestors*.

Table of Contents: *Looking for El Niño* is the name of the Aleut sculptor Bill Prokofiev's whimsical artwork shown here gracing the courtyard of Santa Fe's Institute of American Art Museum.

Cover: The exterior of historic Martinez Hacienda near Taos is adorned with *ristras* of chile peppers and Native American pottery and artifacts.

To all
Native Americans
past and present

CONTENTS

INTRODUCTION

THE OLD WAYS ARE NOT ENTIRELY LOST. THE ANCIENT PEOPLE OF NORTH AND SOUTH AMERICA are mere shadows of the land, but their ghost images are transcendent and haunting skeletons of Machu Picchu's majestic sky cities, hidden sanctuaries of Mayan kings, canyons of giant Pueblo cities at Chaco, and coiling serpents of Ohio—all whispering loudly across the veils of time. Their nagging sighs jangle us—we magnificent masters of harnessed technology. Did they know something we don't?

Humble fiber sandals and broken pottery shards have endured brilliantly, discarded and forgotten, along with the dazzling gold earrings and nose plugs that dulled many European hearts and crippled their souls. Turquoise, coral, and abalone shine deep into the heart. Perhaps these stones are the tears of someone we knew long ago.

We caress Earth, and she embraces us. Her gifts are too many to count, too powerful to imitate, sacred beyond imagination. From Earth Mother's bounty and the Great Spirit's

Pueblo *tablita* designs for a female ceremonial headdress are the inspiration for a gateway at an inn in Santa Fe.

Adobe *horno* ovens were developed by Pueblo Indians —with a Spanish influence— to bake bread and other foods. A sampling of Pueblo pottery and Indian corn adorns this scene in Taos, New Mexico.

Opposite: The hallway to the master bedroom in Mabel Dodge Lujan's Taos home displays rare vintage wall paintings and a drum by Taos Pueblo artists.

blessing, our hunger is satisfied and our hearts made strong. We dream of tomorrow's sunrise and offer prayers into the abyss of eternity.

Let us learn from our parents, our ancestors, and our children. Our stories reside in the hearts of our elders, to be kindled anew within each new person and each new ceremony. Thus we renew ourselves and our remembrance. Long ago, the People emerged from the earth, water, and sky. Each clan wandered over many lands and endured hardships before finding their rightful place, their home. Our journeys fill our minds with wonder and fleeting images of beauty and mystery. We long to be joined with the Great Spirit once again.

So let our path to the Great Spirit be guided by unwavering love and respect—may we "walk in beauty," as the Navajo say. We have been blessed with great powers ourselves to bring honor to the world, our people, our families, and ourselves. We are creators, and we are holy.

In our works of art, our music, our stories, and even our homes, let us not forget that harmony belies chaos, love banishes evil, and prayers redeem transgression. We will worship and honor animals and all living things whose sacred energy sustains us. Nature's power is revealed to us in awesome displays of thunder, lightning, and wind— in the incomparable shades of lavender, copper, and rose she wears in her sunset shawl.

Let us learn these secrets from Native people who still cling fast to a natural way of life. Through their knowledge and insight, we can hope to regain a silent language whispered by the ancients.

In time, we can learn to talk with Earth Mother and the Great Spirit in a native dialect perhaps strange and perhaps familiar.

LEGACY OF ANCIENT AMERICA

THE UNBOUNDED SPLENDOR OF NATURE'S VERDANT MANTLE ON THE BOSOM OF TWO great continents once sprawled as far as the horizon and beyond. Some parts of the Americas remain this way, though much suffers beneath the all-too-familiar glaze of asphalt and concrete.

This modern world, seemingly devoid of concern for nature, could not be the dream of the future foretold by the ancients in their vision quests. The wisdom of the land was a secret known to all tribal peoples of America. From tiny wild corncobs they cultivated maize — the sacred life giver and, for many Native Americans, still the source of ritual worship and artistic inspiration. Peruvian potatoes, Aztec chocolate, wild cotton, Brazilian rubber, and many other natural products first discovered and used by Native Americans are now common household products around the world. The legacy of ancient America weighs

A traditional *horno*, or bread oven, is embraced by a graceful, adobe, stepped half wall at the historic Taos Pueblo.

This spectacular archaeological discovery made twenty years ago is a row of haunting stone idols found at the Aztec Templo Mayor, or main temple.

Opposite: Strings of chile *ristras* and baskets are frequent companion pieces in decorating Native American style.

Following page: Tribute to My Grandmother Mary Ebbets Anislaga, a Chilkat-style blanket by Kwakiultl artist George Hunt, Jr., evokes the Pacific Northwest tradition of carved cedar masks through the sacred tribal representations of bear, lynx, sea monster, and raven. The blanket tells the story of how mankind was taught to weave.

Following page: These pottery vessels represent the Acoma tradition with distinctive geometric designs. The bear is also a traditional symbol used in Acoma pottery.

heavily on the heart and consciousness. It is only relatively recent in global history that the wandering tribes switched from a lifestyle of hunting and scavenging, wandering from familiar campsites to winter havens, to a pattern of village life, and only recently has the true splendor of ancient American cultures been revealed. Spanning a period of about three thousand years, from 1500 B.C. to A.D. 1500, the great Indian civilizations of the Americas blossomed, reached a glorious pinnacle of achievement, then faded away. From the cradle of Mesoamerican culture in central and southern Mexico and Guatemala, the Olmec, Teotihuacán, Mayan, Toltec, and Aztec cultures cast their seeds of cultural influence over great expanses of space and time.

The influence of these cultures is still evident in contemporary Native American design, a design that is multidimensional and dynamic, freely expressing and juxtaposing with timeless icons and motifs of ancient cultures along with state-of-the-art twenty-first-century products. Consequently, a Navajo weaver incorporates imagery such as a United States flag or a Ford pickup truck in her rug, Pueblo potters reincorporate Anasazi designs and techniques, and Santa Fe furniture craftsmen make bed frames inspired by Aztec feathered headdresses.

Three thousand years before white men arrived in the Americas, Indian cultures had touched the sun and moon and stained the soil with rivers of blood in their honor. This mysterious and astonishing American legend is now slowly coming into focus and serves as a prologue to the more familiar Native American design, which has captured the imagination and admiration of millions around the world.

Ancient Americans knew no national or political boundaries other than the geographic realm of a neighboring king or the homeland of a rival clan. Native traders and entrepreneurs ranged far and

wide across the North American continent, and cultural cross-pollination was a natural occurrence. Archaeologists have found brilliant quetzal feathers from southern Mexico in southwestern Anasazi ruins alongside fine jewelry fashioned from Pacific seashells. Prehistoric southwestern pottery shards have been found in Kansas and Ohio.

Since the dramatic entry of European culture into the Americas five centuries ago, Native Americans have influenced design and maintained the lofty traditions of excellent handcraftsmanship and inspired artistic creativity. These values have been passed down from generation to generation, artisan to apprentice, from the beginnings of native expression in the Americas thousands of years ago.

THAT OUR EARTH MOTHER
MAY WRAP HERSELF
IN A FOURFOLD ROBE OF
WHITE MEAL:
THAT SHE MAY BE COVERED
WITH FROST FLOWERS;
THAT YONDER ON ALL THE
MOSSY MOUNTAINS
THE FORESTS MAY HUDDLE
TOGETHER WITH THE COLD;
THAT THEIR ARMS MAY BE
BROKEN BY THE SNOW,
IN ORDER THAT THE LAND MAY
BE THUS,
I HAVE MADE MY PRAYER
STICKS INTO LIVING BEINGS.
— OFFERING: ZUNI

Before Columbus, the Native peoples of the Americas formed a great family of five hundred nations, each boasting unique cultural and design motifs. From this vast resource, contemporary Native American design is constantly inspired and nourished. These motifs, legends, and figures buried beneath a veil of silt, sand, and memory now speak.

An ancient Zuni rock painting.

Opposite: A Pueblo Indian deer dancer in ceremonial headdress performs at Gallup's Inter-Tribal Indian Ceremonial.

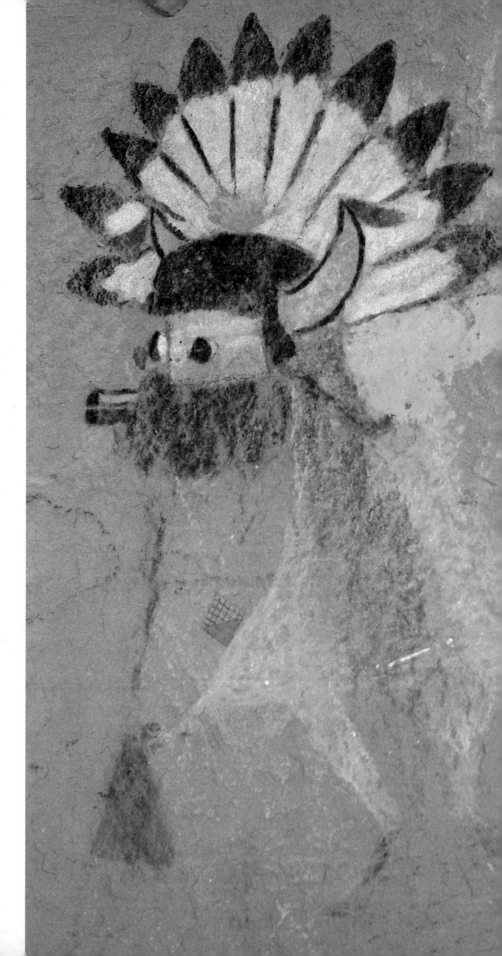

HONORING THE GREAT SPIRIT

There is an old Crow legend that relates, "In the beginning, the first people were lost, poor, and naked. They did not know how to live. Their maker, Old Man, said, 'Go to sleep and get power and whatever animal friends appear in your dreams, pray and listen.' That was how the first people got through the world—by the power of their dreams and with the help of their friends."

The potent power of such dreams and vision quests forms the genesis and creates the genius of contemporary Native American art and design. The influences that inspire Native American designers are rooted in their own past, in a reverence for nature and animals and a strong belief that every part of the earth is sacred.

To Native Americans, the land has always been a living, benevolent, and healing force. And nature, with its changing seasons, has always been a bountiful provider for all of life's

This modern canvas and lodgepole tipi nestles in a pristine mountain landscape on the outskirts of Aspen, Colorado.

Sacred Pueblo clown figures, including mudheads and striped *koshares*, were found at Santa Fe's Indian Market.

Opposite: Old Zuni Pueblo (circa 1912) was a perfect expression of organic architecture. Utilizing natural materials, it was sensitive to the demands of its sometimes harsh climate. Cubical and curved earthen forms create lyrical beauty.

necessities. Whether from nomadic tribes or highly developed social orders such as the Anasazi, they lived in perfect balance and harmony with nature. This belief in equipoise and the nourishing power of the Great Spirit is the underlying foundation upon which all native visions are accepted and believed. In the Native American culture, art and life intertwine. Theirs is a tradition-laden society that was born in the crucible of adversity yet was nurtured by their steadfast communion with nature and inherent belief in its spirit of renewal.

Native Americans initially saw the world holistically, a world whose reality was greater than the sum of its interdependent parts. The authors of *As in a Vision: Masterworks of American Indian Art* state:

> To understand the art of holistic peoples requires a holistic view. Objects made by American Indians whose systems of aesthetics are foreign to non-Indians are nonetheless consistent and sophisticated. These works provide a multi-faceted window through which we can glimpse the life of the societies that made them.
>
> In doing so, we journey into a world where an object's definition depends on its context, not on an arbitrarily ascribed function. A pipe bag might be treated as an element of costume, or as an indicator of its owner's wealth, but during religious events it became the semi-sacred housing of the pipe. Immutable definitions were rare in native North America.

Native Americans' visions often come to them in the silence of the moment when they greet the morning sun or in dreams. These visions are singular, even though they are usually carried out in the hum of studios where craftsmen work with painstaking diligence to form the creations of these visionary dreams. Walking in beauty and harmony with the earth and its creatures is often the leitmotiv of their work.

Their inspirations come from the sensuous, undulating curves or jagged edges of the Southwest mountain ranges. They are inspired by rocks and canyons that rise out of the landscape with drama and mystery, by rivers that wind their way through the landscape, by

meadows ablaze with wildflowers and chamisa, by the eternal magic of the sun and moon, and by the rhythm of the ever-changing seasons.

The genesis of Native American art was humble, often seemingly primitive. Baskets were woven from roots, twigs, or tree branches. Utilitarian bowls and vessels were shaped from the earth's

Navajo women from the Ramah Chapter Weavers Cooperative produced this dazzling display of textile art.

clay then hardened by nature's fire. Pouches were fashioned from hides embroidered with porcupine quills or mallard feathers or painted with colors drawn from nature's plants and berries. Through the simplicity of their art these craftsmen practiced values of economy and natural conservation and expressed their mutual dependency upon an intimacy with nature.

Mountains and canyons became inspired sites for architecture as the Native Americans created sacred places of their own—tipis and pueblos, hogans and lodges—places where families and traditions were nurtured—places of the heart, mind, and spirit that became ceremonial shrines for prayer, meditation, and remembrances.

Within these natural settings they were able to create the funda-
mental elements that are the hallmarks of Native American design—
pottery and textiles, carvings and beaded artifacts, furniture and
accessories, toys and musical instruments—all crafted from the gifts
and inspirations nature so generously provides.

The work of these artisans and craftsmen is romantic, eclectic,
evocative, diverse—a collage of the past and the present, often with
allusions to the future. From history they draw on such classical
forms as Chippendale, Shaker, Art Deco, Biedermeier, Spanish,
Mission, Gothic, Moorish, and Modernism. To those influences they
add their own training (much of it classical), their life experiences,

Lustrous beadwork was
lovingly crafted by a Kiowa or
Comanche mother on a
buckskin baby carrier (about
1900) now a treasure of the
Panhandle Plains Museum
collection.

their religion, and the progressive technology of the high-tech society in which we all live.

Even those artisans who still live in the time warp of the ancient pueblos, sans modern amenities, are touched by the constant encroachment of contemporary life as defined by the computer age of the approaching twenty-first century.

These artisans and craftsmen are ever restless, ever searching to extend the boundaries of creativity in their quest for new designs, materials, processes, or fresh interpretations for old themes, resulting in a wider representation of Native American imagery and influences.

They work in time-honored materials: indigenous woods, wrought iron, tin, stucco, tile, and weavings made from the luxurious wool of the Spanish churro sheep. They add steel, glass, and chrome to create furnishings and accessories that are classical and whimsical, timeless and theatrical.

Adornment has always been the essence of Native American culture. With a respect for nature and all of its living creatures, and a belief in their consummate power, Native American artisans created a language of symbolic hieroglyphics that still holds meaning today. Through the festive embellishment of themselves, their tipis, and the functional and ceremonial trappings of their culture, they found a common ground in the power of art and artistic adornment.

Like the rivers that snake through their terrain, they use recurring symbols—those historical motifs from their compelling legends to add drama, charm, and humor to pottery and baskets,

rugs and blankets, and even the toys and games perceived as having special powers.

The arrows they used for hunting food and killing predators—animal and human—become part of a geometric pattern gracing utilitarian and ceremonial objects. Circles, reminiscent of bird nests and tipis, reveal their belief that life is a continuum. Dancers circle objects in an almost hypnotic repetition. Snapping turtles, bears, buffalo, horses, and lizards fulfill the role of metaphor in their art.

The Inn of the Anasazi library in Santa Fe, New Mexico, has a natural warmth and earthiness.

Opposite: The paintings of Joseph Henry Sharp, 1859–1953, represent a link between the earliest art of the West, the realistic recording of Indian life epitomized by the work of George Catlin, and the latest—the representation of western subject matter in modernist style that began in Taos in the early twentieth century and is still going on today. He was one of the founding members of the Taos Society of Artists. This painting, *Green Corn Ceremony*, is included in the permanent collection of the National Cowboy Hall of Fame.

The buffalo is one of their most important symbols. From birth to death, the animal touched their lives. Hides provided shields, drums, and ropes as well as shelter, warmth, and, at death, shrouds. Horns became drinking vessels and bones were sharpened into knives and other implements. Hooves became rattles for sacred dances.

These objects incorporate centuries-old native traditions. Many objects feature design elements representing significant rites of passage in the Native American culture. From protective charms, amulets, and powerful talismans, these cultural symbols are reinterpreted in new forms.

THEIR ARTISTIC HERITAGE

Native Americans have provided frontier artists and illustrators with a compelling subject for artistic inquiry for as long as Benjamin West has been painting scenes of early American history. In the first part of the nineteenth century, portraits of Native American leaders, who traveled to Washington, D.C., to negotiate treaties, began to inform the American public of the lives of our indigenous populations.

Only a few years after Lewis and Clark trekked across the continent and long before such well-known artists as Charles Wimar and Alfred Jacob Miller discovered them, Native Americans had become consistent art topics.

But George Catlin ranks at the top for setting the stage for America's early understanding of Native American culture. He was mesmerized by their dress, language, and the glimpse they offered into a culture foreign to most of America.

Michael Duty, former director of the Eiteljorg Museum in Indianapolis, Indiana, says, "Catlin began a lifelong quest to capture on

canvas the totality of North American Indian culture in the 1830s after having seen a small delegation of tribal leaders in Philadelphia."

But as author Joan Carpenter Triccoli notes in *First Artist of the West*:

Everything George Catlin did had been done before by someone, in some way. But Catlin made a singularly compelling advance on his predecessors. He was the first artist to devote his entire career—indeed, his entire life—to the West.

Catlin visualized the West for a vast international audience. Without Catlin the entire subsequent history of the art of the American West could not have been the same. Catlin was keenly aware, as would be those who came after him, that the acculturation of American Indians was accelerating. He and later artists of the West were convinced that, in proportion as Indians shed their traditional customs, they diminished in value to the artist in search of authentic subject matter. From the start, Catlin's was a retrospective enterprise; he provided a foundation for the nostalgic tone so endemic to western art.

The 1830s were a momentous decade in American Indian affairs. The aggressive expansionist agenda of the Jackson administration resulted in the displacement of thousands of Indians from the Midwest and Southeast to territory in present-day Kansas, Missouri, and Oklahoma. The consequences were enormous for the indigenous tribes in those areas as well as those uprooted from their homes.

His successors among Indian painters—Seth Eastman, John Mix Stanley, Alfred Jacob Miller, Charles Wimar, George Caleb Bingham, Henry H. Cross, Joseph Henry Sharp, Elbridge Ayer

According to Joan Carpenter Triccoli, author of *First Artist of the West—George Catlin Paintings and Watercolors,* "The buffalo chase on horseback was the height of western sport. Buffalo running furnished physical challenge, danger, and excitement in thrilling concert to Indian and white hunters alike. It was not, however, the most productive way to hunt buffalo; winter hunts—when cows and bulls were separated and their escape was impeded by snow—yielded better harvest." This painting, *Buffalo Chase*, was signed and dated by Catlin in 1847. The painting is part of the permanent collection at Gilcrease Museum in Tulsa, Oklahoma.

Burbank, and Edward S. Curtis—recorded a multitude of subjects. After Catlin, productivity became a measure of a western artist's dedication and importance.

Karl Bodmer's depictions of the Native American culture were a companion to *Travels in the Interior of North America, 1832–1834,* written by the Austrian prince Maximilian. Bodmer produced 400

watercolors, pencil sketches, and field notes that provided a historical, anthropological, and ethnographic viewpoint. An exhibition cat-
alog titled *Karl Bodmer: Engravings from an Expedition*, published for a
Bodmer exhibit in Santa Fe, noted:

> *In illuminating the haunting natural beauty, which aided in the*
> *interior of North America at the time, Bodmer's work, like a sentient*
> *candle in the dark, continues to surprise and delight us. It causes us to*
> *look with new eyes at a pristine America—the raw freshness of its flora*
> *and fauna, its verdant river bottoms, its limpid intercontinental water-*
> *ways, its landscapes which extended as far as the eye could see on either*
> *side of the broad Missouri River.*

His work was founded on the romantic view exemplified by the
European artists Turner, Delacroix, and Friedrich. But his realism
and faithful record of detail characterized the just-emerging art of
photography. On his canvases, he managed to render superb portraits
of Native Americans, often adorned in their most exquisite finery,
with haunting accuracy and a multitude of ethnological details.

Seth Eastman's portrayals were different because he actually
lived among the Indians in the mid-1830s and 1840s. According to
Seth Eastman: A Portfolio of North American Indians, the American
landscape and the American Indian became important to Eastman in
his dual career as a military officer and an artist. During this time,
the army sent him to Florida, Minnesota, and Texas, exposing him to
different remote regions, which involved him in contact with Indian
tribes. He established an identity as the "pictorial historian of the
Indian." His descriptive watercolor and oil illustrations, perhaps

This painting, *Eskimo Tea Time*, by Bettina Steinke of Santa Fe, New Mexico, represents a period in the mid-1950s when the artist had the opportunity to profile many Aleutians and reveal their traditions and ceremonies on canvas. "I fell in love with the Eskimos," Steinke says. "They had great faces and dress. It gave me an opportunity to show the important role fur trading played in the opening of our northwest territories."

better than the work of Catlin and Bodmer, revealed the architectural nuances of the culture and its artifacts.

What Catlin and his successors presented to the world was a white man's view of the Native culture. Aside from petroglyphs and cave drawings, it would not be until the aftermath of the Red River War in 1875 that Native Americans would present to the world their own view of their culture.

Monroe Tsa-Toke was one of the members of the Kiowa 5, whose art was first introduced to an appreciative world public in 1929 with the publication of a portfolio titled Kiowa Indian Art. This painting, *Kiowa and Comanche*, is a casein on paper and is part of the Arthur and Shifra Silberman Collection at the National Cowboy Hall of Fame. Kiowa field matron Susie Peters and Dr. Oscar Jacobson, Dean of the School of Art at the University of Oklahoma in Norman, were instrumental in encouraging the work of the Kiowa 5.

THE ROLE OF LEDGER ART

It was during this time that the federal government decided to exile without trial some of the alleged ringleaders of the rebellion and other Indian warriors accused of depredations and major crimes.

James Auchiah, 1906–1975, was also among the members of the Kiowa 5. This painting, *Dancing Chief*, a tempera on paper, was completed in 1933. Other members were Jack Hokeah, Stephen Mopope, Spencer Asah, and Monroe Tsa-Toke. The painting is part of the Arthur and Shifra Silberman Collection at the National Cowboy Hall of Fame.

Cheyenne painter and sculptor Dick West served as chairman of the art school at Bacone College in Muskogee, Oklahoma, from 1947–1970. Under his direction, the school of art was among the first in the United States where Native Americans were taught the basics of color and design and were also encouraged to incorporate and record their tribal culture within their work.

The late collector and archivist Arthur Silberman wrote:

While their women wailed in mourning, seventy-two demoralized and despondent prisoners in manacles and chains were loaded into wagons for the first leg of their long and arduous journey to the Army prison in the ancient Spanish fortress in St. Augustine, Florida, and the old stone laboratory at Fort Marion, Florida. Everything they had cherished had been swept away by the juggernaut of America's westward expansion. Their future, personal and tribal, appeared dark and foreboding.

Despondent, they asked to paint. With no tipis to decorate, the guards gave them ledger books on which they memorialized their past life in visual form.

They quickly learned trading those ledger drawings could yield better accommodations.

Within weeks of their arrival at Fort Marion, Army Captain Richard Pratt was solicitous and caring. He believed, simplistically, that with education and employment opportunities, Native Americans could immediately be assimilated into mainstream America. His was a bold, albeit flawed, cross-cultural experiment. Pratt ran Fort Marion more like a school than a prison. In this environment the Natives were exposed to a host of doctors, scientists, writers, artists, teachers, statesmen, and churchmen who took an interest in their welfare.

The hope and optimism that characterized the Fort Marion experience was manifest in the innovative and creative works of art produced by several of the prisoners. Most nineteenth-century Indian paintings chronicled individual and tribal martial accomplishments and the

Wah-pah-nah-yah
(Dick West)

MY BROTHERS, THE INDIANS
MUST ALWAYS BE REMEMBERED
IN THIS LAND. OUT OF OUR
LANGUAGES WE HAVE GIVEN
NAME TO MANY BEAUTIFUL
THINGS WHICH WILL ALWAYS
SPEAK OF US. MINNEHAHA
WILL LAUGH AT US, SENECA
WILL SHINE IN OUR IMAGE,
MISSISSIPPI WILL MURMUR
OUR WOES. THE BROAD IOWA
AND THE ROLLING DAKOTA
AND THE FERTILE MICHIGAN
WILL WHISPER OUR NAMES TO
THE SUN THAT KISSES THEM.
THE ROARING NIAGARA, THE
SIGHING ILLINOIS, THE
SINGING DELAWARE, WILL
CHANT UNCEASINGLY OUR
DTA-WA-E (DEATH SONG).
CAN IT BE THAT YOU AND
YOUR CHILDREN WILL HEAR
THAT ETERNAL SONG WITHOUT
A STRICKEN HEART? WE HAVE
BEEN GUILTY OF ONLY ONE
SIN — WE HAVE HAD
POSSESSIONS THAT THE WHITE
MAN COVETED. WE MOVED
AWAY TOWARD THE SETTING
SUN; WE GAVE UP OUR HOMES
TO THE WHITE MAN.
— KHE-THA-A-HI, OR EAGLE WING

Acee Blue Eagle, 1907–1959, a Creek/Pawnee from Oklahoma, was the first art director at Bacone College in Muskogee from 1935–1938, followed by Woody Crumbo, a Creek/Pottawatomie from

1938–1941. Blue Eagle, also an historian, was among Oklahoma Native American artists whose work sold well from 1930–1950 and influenced countless other Native artists across America. This painting, *War Dancer with Fan*, circa 1934, is part of the Arthur and Shifra Silberman Collection at the National Cowboy Hall of Fame.

pageantry of their warrior society ceremonies. Such art was by nature conservative and bound by numerous pictorial conventions. Innovations were slow and gradual.

Native American scholar Dr. Rennard Strickland says:

The ledger drawings of the nineteenth century are without parallel as are the early works of the Kiowas' painting movement and the spectacular Southwest murals. The Arthur and Shifra Silberman Collection, at the National Cowboy Hall of Fame, provides a chronological mirror, not only of the Indian, but of the broader cultural and philosophical issues of Indian society.

Arthur's early life was spent in the shadow of the Nazi twisted cross. He knew firsthand that the genocidal impulse was not unique to any race or any people. His collection is a rich testimonial to the universal need and power to create an art that speaks to survival of the human spirit.

THE ROLE OF THE KIOWA FIVE

As important to an understanding of the historical influences that shaped the work of contemporary craftsmen is an appreciation for the Kiowa Five. James Silverhorn's brother had been among the Fort Marion prisoners, and he shared his artistic insights with his brother. At the turn of the twentieth century, they furthered their artistic heritage by producing tipis, calendars, paintings, and ceremonial equipment.

By the late 1920s, Susie Peters, a Kiowa field matron, and Dr. Arthur Jacobson, dean of the School of Art at the University of Oklahoma, recognized this style of art as unique and singled out five

T. C. Cannon, 1946–1978, was a unique artist among Native Americans who gave the art world a new view of the West. His talent combined the wry humor so distinctive to Indian culture with modern techniques influenced by German Expressionists, the Kiowa 5, and great thinkers of the western world to produce an unusual blend of traditional yet contemporary images. This painting, *His Hair Flows Like a River*, is part of the Arthur and Shifra Silberman Collection at the National Cowboy Hall of Fame.

talented artists to nurture. All were descendants of medicine men or former chiefs. The group included Spencer Asah, Jack Hokeah, Monroe Tsa-Toke, Stephen Mopope, and James Auchiah. The 1929 publication of a portfolio titled *Kiowa Indian Art* was a turning point in the genre that epitomized the Plains Indian style. Their paintings mirrored their world of singers and dancers, ceremonies, and friends.

THE TAOS ART COLONY AND THE TAOS SOCIETY OF ARTISTS, 1911

Only a decade earlier, a group of highly trained and talented artists discovered northern New Mexico and formed the Taos Society of Artists. They were not only struck by the rare quality of light but by the Natives of the area.

Michael Duty observed:

> *Here were Indian cultures that were vastly different than what had been previously pictured in American art. These were people whose culture had remained in place for centuries, who were not nomadic warriors, and whose religious beliefs were quite different from the peoples of the plains and mountains of the northern West.*

Taos artists, such as Sharp, E. I. Couse, Ernest Blumenschein, Victor Higgins, Bert Phillips, and Walter Ufer, presented a new image of Native America to a wide audience. Those images transformed the ways in which Native culture has been portrayed ever since.

THE DOROTHY DUNN STUDIO

Also during this time, Jack Hokeah's ten-year friendship with famed potter Maria Martinez was pivotal to the wider acceptance of Native American art and crafts. Joan Frederick, author of *T. C. Cannon: He Stood in the Sun*, said:

E. Irving Couse, a founding member of the Taos Society of Artists, painted the Native Americans in New Mexico for more than thirty years. This painting, *The Weary Hunter*, as well as *The Sand Painter*, are both part of the Taos Collection at the National Cowboy Hall of Fame.

Hokeah's friendship with the other Kiowa Five members intertwined
professionally and personally among his other artists and friends from
the Southwest Pueblos. In 1932, he participated in an intertribal mural

project for a new arts and crafts building at the U.S. Indian School in
Santa Fe that ultimately led to the foundation of the famous Studio
organized by Dorothy Dunn.

It became a highly acclaimed training program for traditional Native American art, with mostly pueblo tribes attending, but several talented Indian artists, including Allan Houser, also participated. The Studio was the hotbed of creativity in the 1930s Native American art world.

OTHER MERGING INFLUENCES

Two other Oklahoma programs were influential in broadening the awareness of Native American art during the 1930s and 1940s. Bacone College in Muskogee began an art program focusing on Native Americans. Noted painter/historian Acee Blue Eagle, a Creek/Pawnee, was Bacone's first art director from 1935 to 1938, followed by Woody Crumbo, a Pottawatomie/Creek, from 1938 to 1941. Cheyenne painter/sculptor Dick West, who was trained in European art methods, was chairman from 1947 to 1970. During this time, Bacone was one of the few art schools in the United States where Native Americans were encouraged to incorporate their tribal culture within their work.

From the 1950s through the 1970s, Philbrook Museum of Art in Tulsa, Oklahoma, was a catalyst in promoting the talents of Native Americans. By staging an annual juried show, Indian artists from all over the country competed for cash awards in categories relating to their geographic and tribal regions.

Two other events in the 1950s made the world take notice of Native American talent. Dr. Oscar Jacobson produced another portfolio of new Indian talent, and the *National Geographic* sparked interest by publishing Blackbear Bosin's spectacular painting titled

The late-Oklahoma artist Mirac Creepingbear painted in a decidedly contemporary style, yet his work had a definite Indian edge in both form and content. This painting, titled *The Miracle*, shows that special bond between mother and child that is universal in many cultures.

42

Prairie Fire. A commercial artist, Bosin was the first Indian artist to use an airbrush, a technique that aided his already dramatic style.

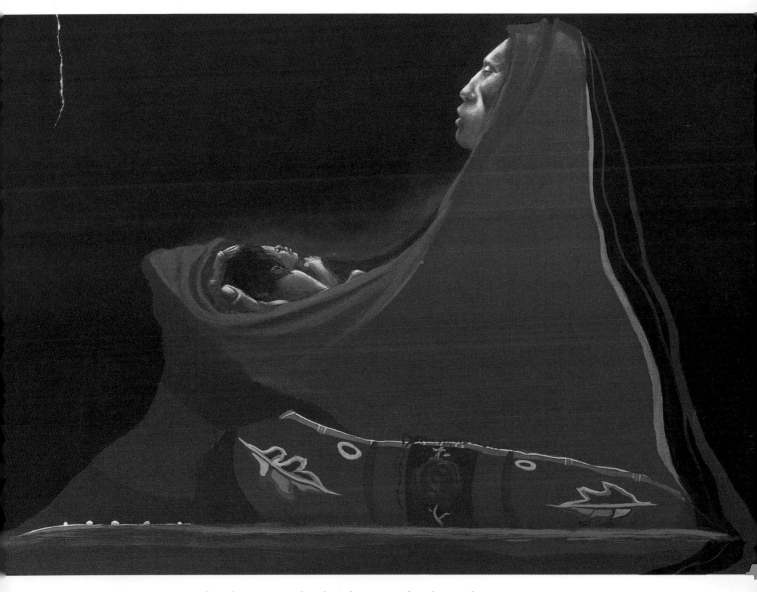

Oscar Howe was considered avant-garde when he painted Indian subjects in a cubist style.

In the 1960s, the Institute of American Indian Arts in Santa Fe took fledgling high-school and college students from all over the

THIS COVERS IT ALL,
THE EARTH AND THE MOST
HIGH POWER WHOSE WAYS
ARE BEAUTIFUL.
ALL IS BEAUTIFUL BEFORE ME,
ALL IS BEAUTIFUL BEHIND ME,
ALL IS BEAUTIFUL BELOW ME,
ALL IS BEAUTIFUL ALL
AROUND ME.

THIS COVERS IT ALL,
THE SKIES AND THE MOST
HIGH POWER WHOSE WAYS
ARE BEAUTIFUL.
ALL IS BEAUTIFUL.
—CHANT: NAVAJO

United States and taught them a mix of classical art history and cutting-edge, innovative technology.

Joan Frederick noted:

> The combination reacted to produce an explosion of creativity unprecedented in Native American art history that began to depict Navajos on buses, abstract fields of color, installation pieces attached to walls, and plays that assaulted controversial issues. Sherman Chaddlesone, Ben Harjo Jr., Parker Boyiddle, Ben Buffalo, Mirac Creepingbear, Richard Ray Whitman, and T. C. Cannon gained national attention by wrestling awards from traditional Native American strongholds. The traditional flat, stylized imagery perpetuated by their ancestors since before the demise of the buffalo was challenged by this new art that echoed the modern world.

Electric colors, combinations of mixed media, and expressionistic methods marked their work. Frederick said:

> It became a new movement in its own right, and to this day, fuels the most successful artists in the economy of the contemporary Native American art scene. Among the artists who held to the traditional style of painting during this volatile period from 1960 to 1980 were Rance Hood, Jerome Tiger, Archie Blackowl, Doc Tate Nevaquaya, Ruthe Blalock Jones, Dennis Belindo, and Leonard Riddles.

> These artists speak their native tongues with the latest tools of modern technology. Though they walk far beyond the steps their ancestors made, they still possess the skills genetically engineered into their culture that allows them to adapt and survive.

And always, their work honors the guiding hand of the Great Spirit.

Vibrant colors are a hallmark of Ray Swanson's paintings of Navajo life. This oil, titled *The Colors of Navajo*, shows Swanson's talent for capturing the beauty and texture of Navajo fabrics. Long a collector of Native American fashions, Swanson often takes Indian heirloom clothes with him to the reservation, posing contemporary models in antique Native American dress.

INSPIRING OTHER CREATORS:
NATIVE-INSPIRED DESIGNS FOR THE HOME

WHAT CONTEMPORARY NATIVE AMERICAN ARTISTS AND CRAFTSMEN HAVE GIVEN TO THE GENRE of design is a romantic view of their culture—a perspective influenced by a unique environment that encouraged the art they produce. But today this nostalgic viewpoint is presented with twentieth-century technology, not only by Native designers but also by those who have been inspired by this fascinating culture. What they create now is a modern form of visual, very tactile anthropology.

The noted authority Barton Wright divides Native American art into two categories: traditional and nontraditional, or contemporary. He stated:

Tradition means not so much a clinging to the handed-down mechanical processes of an art or craft, but a state of mind, a belief in the value of ancestral ways. Opposed to tradition is the misused word, 'contemporary,' broadened

This stunning tipi interior was designed by Cassandra Lohr for a client's mountain retreat near Aspen, Colorado.

Ron McGee's "Plains Buffet" represents a romantic approach to cabinetry, imagining the multicultural design process of a Sioux Indian who "discovers" early American cabinetry and adapts it as his own.

Opposite: This alcove in what was formerly Victor Higgins's home is now in the Lumina Gallery in Taos, New Mexico. It is a shrine to Native American design, crowned by a spectacular set of Taos Pueblo knee-length moccasins.

in recent years to mean nontraditional, innovative, or modern rather than occurring at the same time.

The elements of Native American design are born of the past, rooted in tradition, and are often the result of dreams. Anna Lee Walters, author of *The Spirit of Native America: Beauty and Mysticism in American Indian Art*, eloquently defined this spiritual relationship with the creation of art. From a universal perspective of a Native artisan:

> *The images created by my hands are echoes of the dream-voice within me. They are also evidence of my dream-power, because some of my images can be magic used to heal or destroy, though by vocation I am no sorcerer. The images are powerful by virtue of the forces they represent or by what material and means they came into being.*
>
> *I put a bit of myself into them—my view of the cosmos into a basket, my fingerprint upon a pipe bowl—though you cannot see it. You may simply see isolated, inanimate objects, separated from the spiritual context that inspired their creation. You do not know that I borrowed colors, forms, and materials from a living universe, or that I focused on one haunting image of my dreams, and talking to the image as I worked, it took three-dimensional shape, crawling out of my dreams and the spiritual realm of the universe by its own animal power. The mouth of the carved image opened slowly and spoke; it laughed and sang! Its sculptured legs bent and dashed across the smooth pipe stem.*
>
> *So the ancient, enduring dream-images escaping from my hands are not mine alone to hide and hoard. Living spirits that they are, these things transcend single lifetimes*

and countless generations of spirit seekers. Such powerful
images live lives of their own as I live according to dreams.

It is thus that these creations are born. Beauty and art merge as one spiritual entity and always with a unique aesthetic element that is not separated from the functional aspect of the piece.

The chandelier, with its Native American geometric motif and arrow accents, brightens this kitchen in an Alpine Log Home. Glass-front shelves, a granite countertop, and the slate floor contrast well with the warm glow of the wood cabinetry. A fresh pine bough draped across the window sill, and fresh flowers, fruits, and vegetables, add additional color notes.

Today, at the hands of many of the non-Native designers and craftsmen, the lexicon of design accessories has shifted from an initial utilitarian function to one of adornment and embellishment, not only for the body, but for the dwellings called home. Baskets, vessels, pottery, kachinas, storyteller dolls, masks, musical instruments, toys and games, weavings, rugs, blankets, jewelry, and costumes all now function in a dual role and in a variety of environments as wall or floor art or interior-design accessories.

Like the Mission style, which seemed dormant for almost half a century and to some extent the rustic melting pot of western style, the rhythm, balance, and symmetry of Native American design combine indigenous materials with the simplicity and purity of inspired craftsmanship and futuristic technological innovations. The references to the future are often found in the new space-age materials, new processes, and, of course, new marketing techniques that employ the lightning speed of computer-driven communication methods—all adopted by both Natives and non-Natives. In this milieu of craftsmen who honor old traditions, there is great respect for the power of contemporary commercialism and communication. The maverick holdouts are rare and stubborn breeds.

Today, as people have come to appreciate the rich multilayered diversity of this culture, Native American-inspired designs are revered as a sophisticated genre of their own with as much appeal as other cultural styles. We embrace Native American designs with the same zeal and fervor that we once applied to Mexican and Spanish, European, and oriental themes. In some ways, Native American style has become the elegant chinoiserie of our times.

For some of the non-Native craftsmen and designers, the interest in Native American themes is inspired by a sense of place, or as

writer Rudolfo Anaya calls it, "the spirit of the place." Perhaps their imagination has been sparked by viewing the sacred images of petroglyphs and pictographs on ancient walls and cliffs across the Southwest. Perhaps their cultural memories were tweaked by touring the ancient ruins of Chaco Canyon, Mesa Verde, or the White House Ruin at Canyon de Chelly.

Sans the genetic heritage that Native artisans can claim, the non-Native's interest may have been germinated with a move to places such as Santa Fe, Taos, Sedona, and Flagstaff where they were surrounded by the mysteries and nuances of the culture and were captivated by the romance of its charms. For some, it is a diversion or a response to that perpetual quest for something—a new addition in their artistic repertoire—a way to honor the past and still ride the wave of Native America's present and pervasive popularity. And for some, the genesis of their interest began with something as simple and innocuous as an eight-dollar Native American souvenir.

BASKETS

Natalie F. Linn of Portland, Oregon, a highly respected basket collector, lecturer, consultant, and appraiser, wrote in her master's thesis, "The Artistry of American Indian Basketry":

> *Basketry, a tedious and time-consuming art, has long been the domain of Native American women who often used their front teeth to refine the grasses, before the arrival of the tin can or sharp knives. They were prized for their ability to weave baskets that were not only functional, but oftentimes, a form of currency for their tribe or family. A future husband could look at*

This collection of Papago baskets and Navajo pottery was displayed at a recent Gallup Inter-tribal Indian Ceremonial.

Opposite: An assortment of Apache coiled burden baskets adorned with leather and tin tassels is offered for sale at a recent Santa Fe Indian Market.

BASKETS ARE SMALL
THINGS OF FRAGILE
BEAUTY THAT CAN HOLD
DELICATE SECRETS.
ALL FORMS OF
BASKETRY ARE
WORTH TREASURING.
—NATALIE F. LINN

her teeth and know whether or not a wife would more than add
to the family welfare in trading and selling her wares.

Basketry predates pottery and has been used for every utilitarian function imaginable and woven of every possible indigenous material. Among some materials Linn has encountered are willow, cedar, spruce, maidenhair fern, porcupine quills, and bird feathers. She has even appraised baskets that featured beads pilfered from Catholic rosaries, woven along the rim of the basket. One of the most unusual baskets included quail topknots and feathers from meadowlarks, mallard ducks, and woodpeckers.

Linn stated:

Yet it was not until the white man began developing a
nostalgia for the past that baskets became a valuable

collectible. The period from 1880 to 1930 was called the 'renaissance of basketry' and having an Indian basket to set on one's coffee table became a status symbol—a sign that one was rich enough to have traveled to the West. The Arts and Crafts period also made baskets more desirable.

Tlingit baskets, made by the women of the Tlingit nation in southeastern Alaska, were popular for a century, and by 1890 Alaska had become a favorite spot for tourists to collect Indian baskets. Travel companies often promoted trips throughout Alaska to see the Indians making baskets in their natural habitats.

TRAVELERS THROUGH TIME

Just as tourists became enamored of Alaska and the Pacific Northwest and the Indian baskets they could find there, a similar phenomenon occurred in the Southwest in the early 1900s. It was the height of the railroad era, and the Southwest was being marketed as an exotic vacation destination. We can thank the train, especially the Santa Fe Railway, for much of the acceptance of the artistic trappings of the Native American culture. The train became the matchmaker for America's travelers and Pueblo people with wares to sell, especially pottery. The train and the items purchased on those journeys became symbols of upward mobility to the nation's emerging urban middle classes.

The scene is described aptly in the foreword to *Inventing the Southwest: The Fred Harvey Company and Native American Art*, written by Martin Sullivan, director of the Heard Museum in Phoenix, Arizona:

Hopi artist Madeline Lampson created this superb coiled Yucca basket, which won a top prize at a recent Inter-Tribal Indian Ceremonial in Gallup.

Opposite: Mavis Doering, an award-winning basket maker, blends colors in exquisite circles in these baskets, which are adorned with feathers, suede strings, and silver balls.

A collection of Zuni Pueblo pottery, musical instruments, and headdresses belongs to the famed Olla Maidens, so named for their signature technique of performing with *ollas*, or water pots, balanced atop their heads.

Opposite: Contemporary Pacific Northwest masks are offered for sale at Santa Fe's Indian Market.

A Santa Fe Railway train pauses to take on water during a desert stop in New Mexico. Passengers step off or lean through open windows to examine the fruit, vegetables, and hand-crafted pottery offered for sale by Pueblo families who have gathered from their nearby homes.

This single scene suggests the many transformations in American life that occurred around the turn of the twentieth century. Here is the train itself, no longer a novelty, now a reliable scheduled link between the great cities of both coasts, its rails honeycombing the continent's once-remote interior reaches. Here are the passengers, men and women in the vanguard of the burgeoning middle class, travelers on business or in search of leisurely adventure. And here are the Pueblo people, residents of ancient and long-isolated farming

I PRAY, FRIEND, NOT TO FEEL
ANGRY WITH ME ON ACCOUNT
OF WHAT I ASK OF YOU. TAKE
CARE, FRIEND! KEEP SICKNESS
AWAY FROM ME, SO THAT I MAY
NOT BE KILLED BY SICKNESS OR
IN WAR, O FRIEND!'
—A KWAIKUTL RITUAL PRAYER,
TRANSLATED BY FRANZ BOAS

communities, coming now into daily contact with the cash economy
of urban-industrial America.

The Fred Harvey Company and the Santa Fe Railway joined
forces at an auspicious historical moment. The railroad, the travelers, and the indigenous communities of the region were all integral
elements in a partnership that spanned more than three-quarters of
a century.

While the train provided a new outlet for Native American creativity, Sullivan was quick to note how the railroad also changed life
for Native Americans in less-welcome ways:

> Rail lines sliced through the primeval grazing grounds
> of the Plains, bisecting traditional hunting routes and
> violating the boundaries of treaty land. Trains brought
> would-be settlers who were eager to try their luck on the

This exquisite, carved seed pot in the Santa Clara Pueblo black-pottery style features a sun god with feathered headdress.

Opposite: The spiral is an ancient Anasazi symbol for origin, which is repeated here on an elegant Acoma *olla* and painted on a wall in Santa Fe's Inn of the Anasazi.

patchwork of land grants made by the federal government as inducements to the railroad companies. At the same time, Congress passed the Dawes Act of 1887, which was intended to curtail the reservation system through individual land allotments to Native Americans.

By the turn of the century, many observers were convinced that Native American traditional cultures would not survive in the face of all these changes. . . . American Indians seemed consigned to a mythic past.

What few counted on, though, was the tenacious Native American will to survive the genocide of total acculturation and absorption into the Anglo culture. Their ability to adapt, to create objects of art, and to tap into the mainstream of American entrepreneurship and commercialism is a historical development and a human triumph well worth applauding.

POTTERY-SHARDS OF THE PAST

Native American pottery is distinguished by its infinite variety of shapes, sizes, and ornamentations. Vessels from the Santa Clara Pueblo or the Cochiti Pueblo look vastly different from those created by the potters of San Ildefonso or Acoma. Consider the differences between the gleaming black pots made by Maria and Julian Martinez and those figurative pieces from the heart and hand of Nampeyo, the famous Tewa-Hopi potter who is credited with the revival of fifteenth-century Skiyatki polychrome wares and then influencing her succeeding generations.

Clara Lee Tanner wrote in the introduction to *Beyond Tradition: Contemporary Indian Art and Its Evolution:* "It was in ceramics that the

They say the clay
remembers the hands
that made it.
They say that every
piece of clay
is a piece
of someone's life.
— Byrd Baylor
When Clay Sings

Painted urns nestled in a bed of petunias add summer color and a Native American flair for a storefront display during Santa Fe's Indian Market.

prehistoric Southwestern Indian cultures reaped their richest artistic harvest and left their most valuable tradition."

Native people have been making pottery in the same place, and in the same way for more than 1,500 years. But what wrought these changes in this art form that began with a simple mound of clay? Alexander E. Anthony Jr., writing in the foreword to *Southwestern Pottery: Anasazi to Zuni*, calls it simply "alien influences and market pressures." Those foreign influences changed forever the insular quality of Indian life. He said, "Change first occurred among the tribes as a result of contact with other Indian groups. The Plains Indians influenced the Pueblos and Navajos through trade, as did the Indians of today's Mexico." As the Spanish conquerors impacted their life, Spanish floral, foliage, and lacy motifs crept into the designs on Pueblo pottery. Vessel shapes slowly changed to accommodate the needs of the new arrivals from across the ocean. Then came the railroad three centuries later. Museums began collecting Native American pottery, fearing the imminent demise of this culture. Visitors to the Southwest sought authentic native souvenirs—best known as "curios."

Anthony further noted:

In response, potters produced pots specifically for tourists. At first, they made beautifully decorated replicas of the ones made for their own use. Quickly, they learned they could speed up the process and sell more if they made them smaller. Then they learned they could make even more if they took less time on each piece. The period of magnificent historic pottery came to an abrupt end, and the period of tourist wares began. For the next hundred plus years, market fluctuations shaped Southwestern pottery's development.

Kachinas and other Native American artifacts are displayed on this Cody, Wyoming, antique sideboard.

Opposite: A Wyoming interior sparkles with Native American style, including Pueblo pottery, kachina dolls, and Navajo rugs.

The early 1970s marked a turning point for pottery as artisans broke away from tribal restrictions and wed their own inspirations

with those from other Native American traditions. Experimentation was heightened, even though potters inevitably returned to some semblance of traceries of tradition.

Noted collectors such as Allan Hayes and John Blom claim, however, that:

The 1990s represent a Golden Age in Southwestern pottery. Today's pottery is more carefully made and designed than ever before because pottery manufacturing has always followed the market, and market standards right now are at an all-time high. The market rewards potters who make pieces for discerning collectors and penalizes those who make lesser pieces for casual tourists.

Hayes and Blom believe the appeal of pottery lies in the fact that "the pot you bought last week carries the imprint of long-vanished peoples—the Anasazi, Mogollon, Hohokam, Salado, and Sinagua—whose ruins add magic to the Arizona and New Mexico landscape. They say:

Yet, Southwestern pottery bears all this tradition with a youthful, even frisky, energy. This is its Golden Age, a dazzling turn-of-the-millennium burst of productivity and innovation. Now it's almost a given: next year's work will be better than this year's and the year after, better still. Despite all the creativity, painstaking craft, and historic value, this pottery remains implausibly accessible, more so than any other important art form.

Large water jars called *ollas*, such as this Acoma Pueblo example, have become highly prized by collectors.

Opposite: Elegant Pueblo pottery forms have their source in organic prototypes, such as gourds, squashes, and melons.

Living with a piece of pottery can be an exhilarating experience for the collector. As Hayes and Blom noted, "Many Native American potters tell how deeply moved they are by the process—a combination of bonding with the land and bonding with the past. They see a pot as a living entity rather than as an object."

Artist Maynard Dixon described his life in Hopi land as a life both mystic and real. He once wrote to a friend, "You would suppose that here in the ancient Province of Tusayan that I would have plenty of time for everything. But it is not our kind of time—you can't count on it. It is made only of days, moons, and eternity."

The late John Wayne was an avid collector of Kachina dolls. To him they represented an era and a region he enjoyed. The kachinas reminded him of people with whom he had starred and worked so often in Monument Valley. This one, called *Wakas*, or cow, stands a little over nineteen inches high and is part of the collection John Wayne donated to the National Cowboy Hall of Fame and Western Heritage Center in Oklahoma City, Oklahoma.

Tawa, the Sun Kachina, is painted to reflect the sun's rays, an important part of Native American legend.

Patung, representing a squash or watermelon, is thirteen inches high.

The Hon, or Bear Kachina, is also painted to represent his role in a Hopi ceremony.

All kachinas on these two pages are from the John Wayne Collection at the National Cowboy Hall of Fame.

A mystical spirit is very much a part of the Hopi culture, best known for its intricately carved kachina dolls. Alph H. Secakuku, a Hopi carver and author of *Following the Sun and Moon: Hopi Kachina Tradition*, stated, "The Hopi believe their greatest bond is their religion. It has given them the strength to resist external forces and has kept them united for centuries."

To the Hopi, these symbolic figures are benevolent spirits that include elderly wise chiefs, priests, warriors, leaders, mothers, clowns, dancers. The spirits spend half the year high up in the San Francisco peaks and half with the Hopi on their three mesa-top villages, where they dance and act as spiritual intermediaries to the gods.

The kachina dolls, presented by the dancers, are used to teach the Hopi children to recognize the spirits and understand the all-important seasonal ceremonies of the Hopi tradition. The dolls play a major role, from fertility rituals to blessing the children born

WE DO NOT PERCEIVE THE KACHINA OR KATSINA DOLLS SIMPLY AS CARVED FIGURINES OR BRIGHTLY DECORATED OBJECTS. THEY HAVE IMPORTANT MEANING TO US, THE HOPI PEOPLE; WE BELIEVE THEY ARE PERSONIFICATIONS OF THE KATSINA SPIRITS.
—ALPH H. SECAKUKU
KACHINA CARVER

of those sacred ceremonies. Hand-carved and hand-painted, they are imbued with special powers; so real are their spirits that kachinas are easily viewed by non-Natives as elaborate icons of cultural personification.

Hopi artisans carve the dolls out of cottonwood roots for educational and ceremonial use, but in recent years some dolls have been made specifically for the tourist market. Even fifteen years ago, author Paul Rossi wrote, "Kachina figures of recent origin show the

natural influence of the modern world. Clothing and the elaborateness of the art are influenced by teachers, traders, and other contacts. Kachinas made even prior to 1900 are more primitive in appearance."

Today, kachinas—these creatures of the imagination—are eagerly collected for both their spiritual importance as well as their fine artistic merit. Among the most noted collectors are Barry Goldwater, who gave his collection of 437 Kachina dolls to the Heard Museum in 1975, and John Wayne, who gave his smaller sixty-four-piece collection to the National Cowboy Hall of Fame in the early 1980s.

TEXTILES

Noted scholar of Navajo textiles Charles Avery Amsden wrote in 1935:

Navajo weaving began, if we really want to go down to the roots, long before the Navajo tribe was known in its present location, or had ever learned anything about loom weaving. The Pueblo people, who were the remote ancestors of those living today, first practiced this great craft in the Southwest, using cotton instead of the wool of later times.

Where they learned to cultivate cotton, and spin and weave it, is more than we can say, but it is perfectly plain to archaeologists who find cotton blankets buried with their dead that they were at it at least a thousand years ago and have kept at it down to this day. No trace of the Navajo can be found in those early times, none in fact until almost the time of the Spanish discovery and conquest of the Southwest.

Amsden's scholarly research readily refutes the legend that the Navajo learned to weave from Spider Woman, one of the Holy People who lived atop a pinnacle in Canyon de Chelly.

While early weavings depicted distinct regional characteristics—from the striped chief's blankets of the mid-1800s to the Germantown yarns that yielded more colorful, geometric

THOSE WHO BUY THE ART OF SOUTHWEST WEAVERS ARE BUYING MORE THAN A FUNCTIONAL OBJECT, AN ADORNMENT FOR WALL OR FLOOR. THEY ARE BUYING A FORM OF COMMUNICATION, WHICH TELLS OTHERS OF THEIR AFFILIATION AND AFFINITY WITH THE SOUTHWEST, ITS LIFESTYLE, ITS HISTORY, ITS PEOPLE.
—SUZANNE BAIZERMAN, AUTHOR OF
RAMONA SAKIESTEWA: PATTERNED DREAMS TEXTILES OF THE SOUTHWEST

patterns—today the regional lines are blurred and weavers strive for designs that are more innovative and express their spirit of individuality.

Don Dedera, writing in *Navajo Rugs: How to Find, Evaluate, Buy and Care for Them*, noted:

At a time when the artistic glory of long-vanished tribes lies faded and all but forgotten in museums . . . the

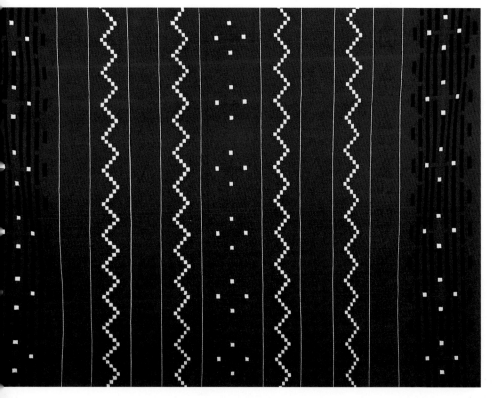

weaving of Navajo artisans is acclaimed around the world. Taken together, according to the U.S. Department of Commerce, Navajo arts and crafts today pump about $15 million annually into the tribal economy. Substantial numbers of those dollars come from Germany, Italy, England, Holland, and France, where Navajo handiwork became popular in interior design during the late 1980s.

The prize-winning rugs of Navajo artist Rena Begay are modern interpretations of traditional designs, such as Two Grey Hills, Chief's Blankets, and this boldly colored Wide Ruins pattern.

Opposite: All manner of Native American collectibles are used as accent accessories in this bold room in a home built by Alpine Log Homes. The rock fireplace with its simple log mantel quickly draws the eye's attention.

Preceding page, left, top: Hands of friendly contact are the theme of Osage artist Wendy Ponca's Wah-sha-she blanket produced for the American Indian College Fund.

Preceding page, left, bottom: After 1880, the railroad brought commodities to Navajo families in the Southwest, including colorful acrylic yarn from mills in Pennsylvania. Weavers responded by creating eyedazzling tapestries.

Preceding page, right, top: An example of a classic Navajo chief's blanket features the signature and contrasting stripes and crosses design and is typical of rugs produced about 1870–1880.

Preceding page, right, bottom: Hopi artist Ramona Sakiestewa has introduced a dramatic new approach in her weavings.

Many dealers agree that the market for Navajo weaving jumped to a new plateau around Christmas 1987.

Dedera quoted Don Garland, whose gallery in Sedona, Arizona, is said to have the largest inventory of Navajo weaves in the world, as stating:

'I believe at about that time a very large number of potential patrons came to look upon Navajo weaving as an emotional expression—not a quaint handicraft. When you touch a Navajo rug, you can feel the weaver in it. It came out of her heart and imagination. When you have one to keep, you know there is not another in the world like it.'

JEWELRY

Seeds, shells, beads, turquoise, coral, metal, wood, bone, and horns—such are the materials from which Native American jewelry is fashioned. But it is turquoise that is considered the gemstone of the West. Its greatest appeal is its surreal resemblance to a vast blue western sky.

Southwestern tribes considered turquoise a talisman of good fortune and used it for ornamental and ceremonial purposes. Apaches tied turquoise beads to guide the flight of their arrows. Navajos used turquoise beads as currency. Zunis believed the blue of turquoise symbolized the origin of life.

Silver, often obtained by melting down United States silver dollars, provided Navajos, Pueblos, and other Indians with the perfect metal to create distinctive turquoise jewelry. Silver's white gleam beautifully complemented the turquoise. Turquoise in silver, often supplemented with red coral, white shell, black obsidian, and other traditional Indian gemstone materials, established the enduring pattern of Native American jewelry.

This award-winning Navajo bracelet shimmers with a design of inlaid jet, turquoise, coral, and mother-of-pearl pieces.

A historic photograph of Zuni jeweler Della Casi shows her in traditional apparel and hairstyle at work on the famous Zuni "needlepoint" designs.

Preceding page: Beautifully detailed with the defining richness of intricate hand stamping, this handcrafted sterling-silver piece is truly tomorrow's heirloom. The box features a lid that is also an impressive buckle set with turquoise and oxblood coral.

Mary Colton's letter planted the seed for Hopi overlay jewelry, which requires two sheets of silver. Her vision led to the formation of the Hopi Silvercraft Guild in 1949; in 1961, Hopicrafts, a private enterprise, opened on the reservation as well. In the 1940s, Waddell Trading Company furthered the work of Native American jewelry designers.

Gene Waddell cites the work of such artists as Charles Loloma, Harvey Begay, and Larry Golsh as pioneering the new traditions of Native American jewelry. In fact, Charles Loloma, a potter and painter, was so on the cutting edge of jewelry design that his work was rejected for a Hopi Indian Fair in the late 1950s; the judges said it was not "Indian" in design. Now he is considered the leader in contemporary jewelry art. The year 1970 marked a turning point for Indian jewelry as a worldwide market sought their innovative designs.

"These artists pioneered the new traditions of Native American jewelry," Waddell said. "Today, many artists use gold or silver and a variety of gemstones, including turquoise, coral, lapis, and even diamonds."

These designs mix silver and other precious stones in contemporary jewelry by Ray Tracey.

Preceding page: Concho belts are a popular fashion accessory for Native American fashions, but they also serve as home decor accents as well. Fashioned of silver, they are often accented with semi-precious stones.

New work combines a variety of techniques and designs that appear architectural in form. Lapidary inlay work is teamed with sandcasting. Gold is set with turquoise and lapis lazuli. Australian opal in bead and cabochon form are set in 14 kg weight.

While tribal and sacred restrictions fostered the original traditional designs, like the blurred lines of weaving, Native and non-Native craftsmen respond today to contemporary influences that cross tribal, geographical, and gender lines, broaden and stretch cultural boundaries, and push their ever-restless imaginations to new artistic heights.

PAINTING

Dorothy Dunn remarked in 1968:

Painting is so much a part of all the arts through which the Indian identifies . . . with the universe that to consider it apart from the whole is like examining a single thread drawn from a tightly twisted cord. One art intertwines with and supplements the others; they all unite to join the Indian and his earth and sky and his unseen gods. Art is a way of life. It has a bearing upon every aspect and detail of the Indian's existence—birth, nourishment, rest, growth, learning, work, play, reproduction, healing, even death.

Painting is very much a part of R. C. Gorman's life. The prominent Navajo artist began painting when he was three years old— sheep, hogans, cowboys, and Indians, even Shirley Temple, one of his favorite child actresses. "By the time I was in the seventh grade at the Ganado Mission School, I was selling some of my work. Back then, they were very traditional Indian paintings," he said in an interview for *Persimmon Hill.*

In 1965, Gorman held his first show in Taos at John Manchester's home and gallery. He invited his whole family, and they arrived in their traditional Navajo dress. Gorman's gallery director, Virginia Dooley, recalled, "Nobody had ever seen Indian art like this. The show was a smash. By 1968, Gorman had purchased Manchester's home, which is now 211 years old, and named it the Navajo Gallery.

He wanted people to know who and what he was and to show his loyalty to the tribe." Gorman's gallery is the first Native American-owned-and-operated gallery in the country.

Even the celebrated Rubenesque women in his paintings are a link to his Native culture. "The model has a lot to do with what comes out on the canvas," Gorman said. "The model sets the mood. I usually have no idea what I will paint until the model walks into the studio." He often uses Native American women of the various tribes as the basis for his voluptuous and sensual women.

Critic Stephen Parks observed:

The women in his drawings and sculpture are the women of his youth, the women who raised him in the remote reaches of the Navajo reservation around Chinle, Arizona. They sum up the strength and grace of the Indian woman and do so eloquently and succinctly.

Most of us in the Southwest are so accustomed to his images that we take them for granted; we forget that it's Gorman's art and his force of personality that have virtually created the archetype that is now universally recognized as the Navajo Madonna. These women are a very real connection with his past and youth.

When asked what he hopes people see in his paintings, Gorman said:

Everybody reacts differently to my work although I don't think people are ever indifferent. I think people find a certain beauty in my work. I think it's been able to stand out for a long time because it has enduring qualities and the subjects of the paintings are good.

Artist Theodore B. Villa expresses a similar albeit more succinct theme. He said, "It's my preference that whoever looks at my

Preceding page: Traditional elements of Southwest and Native American interior design—corbels and vigas—are reflected in this living room and adjacent entry hall. A Moorish influence is seen in the curve of the wall. A collection of Native American pottery fits nicely in the entry-hall niches, and a painting of shamans by Paul Pletke dominates the room.

Opposite: *Seminoles in the Everglades*, a gouache on illustration board, was done by the Creek artist Fred Beaver in 1970. Beaver was born in 1911 and died in 1980. Much of his art revealed the lifestyle of the Seminoles in Florida. The painting is part of the Arthur and Shifra Silberman Collection at the National Cowboy Hall of Fame.

work takes from it what they will. Any statement I make about my work will only inhibit the viewer's response."

Most Native American painters also struggle with the concept of living in two worlds. Harry Fonseca, known for his colorful portrayals of coyotes in modern dress, said:

It's hard to have tradition so close at hand and then have to live in the contemporary world. It's wonderful if you can see both clearly, then you have a balance. Coyote means many things to many people—for me coyote is a survivor and is indeed the spice of life.

Years ago, Armond Lara had to come to grips with that conflict of living in two worlds. She said:

One day I was painting portraits in a very old-world style, and all of a sudden I wondered, what the hell am I doing? This is the way Flemish artists painted. I've never been to Holland. I don't know anything about that way of life. Why am I doing this?

At that point, fortunately, one of my professors, who happened to be Asian, told me, 'You know, you're right. You should do what you know, and what you know seems to have a lot to do with texture.'

Everything turned around for me at that point. Texture is what this whole country's about—Colorado, New Mexico, Texas, Arizona. There's a lot of texture involved. I feel about this part of the world. I feel a relationship about this world, the way of life, and this environment—that's what I know about. I know about dry riverbeds and what they look like after there's been a drought. I know about lizards, and barbed-wire fences, and the color of dawn or sunset. That's what I know about.

Going home is another significant theme running like a melody through many paintings by Native Americans. Jaune Quick-To-See Smith said:

Landscape has occupied my work for a number of years. The subconscious need for 'going home' is a pervasive one for all Indian people. Blocks of color represent range, prairie, aerial view, and plowed land. No matter how I synthesize my perceptions, they are never traditional views of landscape with horizon line and static space. Rather, I

All manner of Native American collectibles are used as accent accessories in this bold room in a home built by Alpine Log Homes. The rock fireplace with its simple log mantel quickly draws the eye's attention. Native American rugs and pillows add textural and color interest, as do the totem pole, blanket ladder, cowboy-boot lamp, and paintings.

FOR NATIVE AMERICAN
CHILDREN, PLAY WAS
ALSO A PREPARATION
FOR LIFE.
—DON AND DEBRA
MCQUISTON,
AUTHORS OF *DOLLS
& TOYS OF NATIVE
AMERICA: A JOURNEY
THROUGH CHILDHOOD*

create habitations with signs, symbols, figures, animals,
tracks, maps, and even constellations, keeping in mind that
the landscape is always full of movement.

The pictograph painting and drawing style I have
developed comes from a study of historical American Indian
artifacts, rock petroglyphs/pictographs, and paintings.
Further, I look for reference between the two worlds, which
seem to carry a similarity in aesthetic qualities.

For instance, color in beadwork shows a clear understanding of the theories of color of Josef Albers's or a Naskapi bag reflects the childlike simplicity of Paul Klee's work. These and other parallels seem as fresh and spontaneous to me as most contemporary art.

Drawing these parallels between the historical Indian art world and that of the contemporary art world is an important support for my work. As I travel and lecture, I encourage other Indian people to look at their historical tribal art in conjunction with their university training.

TOYS AND GAMES

Don and Debra McQuiston, authors of *Dolls & Toys of Native America: A Journey Through Childhood* state that by playing with the miniature dolls, tipis, sleds, spears, canoes, kachinas, and cradle boards made for them by their parents and grandparents, girls and boys learned the skills that would take them into adulthood. In time, they would pass along these skills to their own children and grandchildren.

Once objects of play, these toys have now become objects for ornamentation. Cradle boards and kachinas grace walls the same way European fine art does in some homes. Sleds line fireplaces. Miniature canoes and tipis look comfortably at home on a mantel. Fashion, too, transcends its utilitarian function with beadwork dresses and moccasins that become wall art.

Like other objects that had their birthright in ceremonial events—masks and drums, rattles, pipes, headdresses, and flutes—

A Lakota doll, circa 1915, was a gift to the National Cowboy Hall of Fame from Malcolm Doran Taylor and the Mark Devin Taylor Trust. Artifacts such as these provide information about a society. From powerful abstract designs of beadwork to beautiful wooden sculptural forms and colorful woolen blankets, the First Peoples created visual expressions in their clothing, jewelry, toys, and weapons that reflected their experiences.

Opposite: A playful *koshare*, or clown kachina doll, greets collectors at Santa Fe's Indian Market. It is depicted in the "storyteller" motif, with baby koshares crawling over the mother.

these symbols of power now double as design accessories that reflect an appreciation for these elements of Native American history.

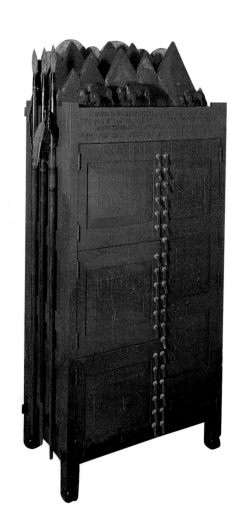

VISIONS FOR THE FUTURE

Ever inquisitive, ever pushing, the Native artisans and the non-Natives they have influenced all share a love of experimentation as they stretch the horizons of their art. They move beyond tribal pressures to stay within traditional thought. They cross gender barriers that were once restrictive. They assimilate ideas and designs from other tribes and other cultures around the world.

But however far they push the edge of creativity, they are ever mindful of the need to respect the heritage and traditions that have inspired their contemporary art. They now exhibit their work in Germany, France, Italy, and Japan. Their work is given as gifts of state. Their art is the source of television documentaries.

As Clara Lee Tanner once stated, "Native art has evolved out of a unity of tradition, transition, and innovation." Especially innovation, paired with the dominant will to reflect the diversity of this unique culture through art.

As Michael Duty noted in an article in *U.S. Art:*

> *The Native American culture has not vanished; it has persisted even in the face of great adversity. The work of Catlin, John Mix Stanley, and Edward Curtis can still be found in museums and galleries today, along with pieces by hundreds of other artists. What's more, art by and about American Indians may well be more prevalent than ever before.*

Why does the Native American influence represent such a strong and far-reaching appeal today? Many think it is because it gives us an opportunity to embrace our oldest culture and to adapt its multidi-

Furniture offered by New West craftsmen of Cody, Wyoming, marries the legendary and rugged appeal of the Molesworth tradition with romantic Native American images.

Opposite: Santa Fe artist, L. D. Burke, designed this "Buffalo" *trastero*, or cabinet, complete with Plains Indian lances, lamenting the vanishing of the great beasts from the prairie.

mensional facets to our own architecture, interiors, and lifestyle. These Native American visions touch everyone's past while giving us a

This room exudes a sturdy, masculine charm with its massive stacked stone Masinter fireplace, the heavy log beams, and the rustic furnishings in the Thomas Molesworth tradition. The sofa is piped in leather cording for an added touch of masculinity. Chandeliers and light fixtures echo the rustic great outdoors theme. The home was designed and built by Custom Log Homes Incorporated of Stevensville, Montana.

Old Indian arrows were used to accent twin mirror frames created by L.D. Burke III, of Santa Fe. A shaded effect was used in the paint treatment to highlight the distressed wooden frames.

Opposite: The rugged character of the West is evidenced in this home and adjoining deck built by Alpine Log Homes of Victor, Montana. The wrought-iron lances form the basis for the chandelier, fashioned of rawhide. A Native American blanket becomes a perfect tablecloth for the informal bar.

vision of the future, and in so doing, they enhance our own understanding of this rich and complex culture and its cycles of life.

Duty said one primary reason for the popularity of all facets of Native American art may be that "the art connects the viewer with a simpler, more direct time. Much of Native American art portrays people who seem intimately in touch with their natural surroundings, in tune with nature, with the land itself and with the changing climate."

Not coincidentally, many contemporary depictions of Native American life are set prior to the white man's settlement of the frontier. Art that reflects that time period and shows people responding to and reverent of the natural rhythms of the earth can have a profound appeal in an age when most people spend much of their time staring at a variety of computer and video screens.

Many Native American artists and those they influence are on a vision quest of their own today. They follow in the footsteps of luminaries both historical and contemporary. Like their ancestors before them, who sought solace and wisdom by embarking on a solitary vision quest, these artisans seek out their own sanctuaries of talent as they search for new techniques and designs that will help them tell, with passion, the story of their culture through art, crafts, and design.

These are designs born of visions that pay eternal tribute to the great spirit of creativity—and to the ability of the human spirit to endure. The fact that these designs now influence non-Natives is perhaps the ultimate tribute to any culture—that we embrace a style outside of our own regional, cultural, and emotional understanding and boundaries and begin to call it our own.

Native American visions offer us a walk through the past that leads us into the future—a tomorrow where an ancient culture, its peoples, and its timeless influences are revered and held in high esteem.

CRAFTSMEN AND DESIGNERS

NATIVE AMERICAN CRAFTSMEN
VIRGINIA STROUD

A CHEROKEE-CREEK TRADITIONAL ARTIST LIVING IN MUSKOGEE, OKLAHOMA, VIRGINIA STROUD knew at age seven she would be an artist. At twelve, she had her first exhibition and by fifteen was winning major regional awards for paintings springing from her imagination and the rites of passage that are important ceremonies in her culture.

Women and children figure prominently in her art, which has been exhibited at Gilcrease Museum in Tulsa, Oklahoma, the Wheelwright Museum in Santa Fe, New Mexico, the Museum of Man in San Diego, California, and the Southern Plains Museum in Anadarko, Oklahoma.

Her early mentors were Fred Beaver, Solomon McCombs, and Donald Vann. Among her contemporaries, she admires the whimsical work of Harry Fonseca, a Taos, New Mexico, artist who turned the coyote into an artistic icon, and Kevin Red Star, who is noted for painting

Navajo women are celebrated in a uniquely stunning bench by Cherokee artist Virginia Stroud at a recent exhibit.

people with big noses and big lips. Always one to listen to her own heart, Stroud says 1987 was clearly a turning point in her career. That was when she began embellishing furniture following what she called a visionary experience on the way home from an art exhibit in Phoenix, Arizona.

"I just heard voices in my head telling me to take my figures from my canvases and let them go onto a different kind of canvas—a wooden bench," she recalls. "Not a functional bench that also holds blankets, just a bench you can sit on and let the figures embrace you."

The benches often feature women sitting together, their backs and legs intricately cut out and painted. Stroud says, "When you sit down on the bench, you are sitting on the women's laps so to speak. That way you are never alone. You are always very close to your angels and spirit guides."

Stroud suffered a great disappointment, however, when a regional museum labeled her work as "cabin craft," not art. On the same day, *Southwest Art* called her seeking her opinion on the topic "Contemporary Art Furniture: Fine Art or Craft?"

Still, Stroud says she allowed herself to be "caged" by one small institution's censorship and stopped making the benches. In 1995, however, the magic of these pieces lured her back to her workroom where she completes every aspect—from cutting out their whimsical shapes with a jigsaw to the final coats of polyurethane.

"I've always been comfortable with my spirit guides," Stroud says. "But it's only recently that people became more accepting of angels and other spirits that help guide them through the passages of

life." Now, these three-dimensional pieces are frequently exhibited and sell for $5,000 to $20,000. "They are also imitated," she adds.

Her newest endeavor is masks drawn from human faces and life forms, using a technique taught to her by Charlotte Carlston, the artist on whom Robert Redford based his movie *Rachel River*. Stroud is also interested in kinetics and envisions several kinetic sculpture projects in her future.

There is a happy quality in Stroud's work. She says, "In my world of art, the sun is always shining, the children are always loved. And it is always spring."

JAMES FERRARA

James Ferrara's Bannock/Shoshone heritage comes into play when he creates rustic western-style furnishings. He is inspired by the traditional elements of native mythology—the sun and moon, buffalo and bleached white skulls—but his interpretation is futuristic.

The shapes of Ferrara's chests, cabinets, and consoles are redolent of mountaintops, half moons, and skulls, calling to mind ancient forms made modern by his craftsmanship. He works with aged pine, fir, spruce, embossed copper, and hides in natural finishes or bold colors drawn from weavings. "I lean to red and purple," he said. An old parfleche can inspire a chest or table. An elk hide can become an innovative backdrop for jewelry.

Working out of his studio in Seattle, Washington, Ferrara brings to his furniture a companion career as an art director and set designer. Many times while dressing a set, the search for the perfect

Opposite and above: Designer James Ferrara draws upon his Bannock and Shoshone ancestry from the Pacific Northwest to create contemporary cabinets that express Native color, themes, and shapes.

prop necessitates his talent for improvisational design. The triangle, a long-respected shape in Native culture, is Ferrara's trademark. "It's the simplest, most efficient engineering shape to use," he said.

ALICE WARDER SEELY

Alice Warder Seely of Hondo, New Mexico, draws on the Mimbres culture, ancient masks, and storyteller dolls to create contemporary, whimsical paintings, sculptures, *tabletas*, jewelry, and handpainted travois boxes. Her partner, native New Mexican David Hall, developed the format for her box designs and assists in the creation of her jewelry.

She brings to her art a rich family lineage. Her maternal grandmothers, Eleanor Brownell and Alice Howland, came to Santa Fe from Philadelphia in the 1930s and were the Santa Fe Opera's first two presidents. Her paternal grandparents, descendants of San Juan and Comanche Indians, were from the small northern New Mexico village of Guadalupita. Her stepfather is the Navajo artist Ha-So-De.

Seely grew up in the company of Santa Fe artists Cyrus Baldridge, Gustav Baumann, and Josef Bakos, and her style is reminiscent of the traditional New Mexican painters of the 1930s and 1940s. Her art is known for its flowing movement and bright dramatic colors. But the greatest influences are "my love of New Mexico

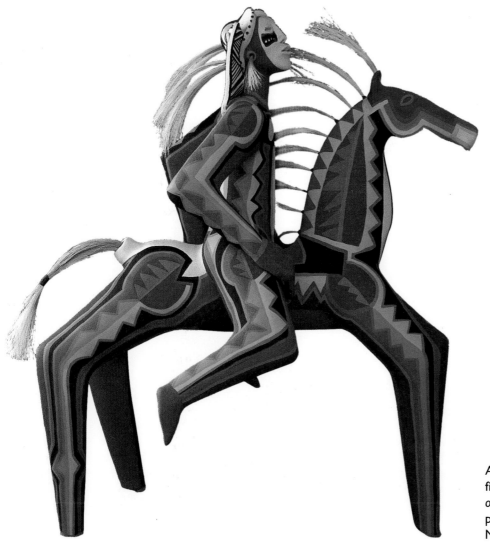

Alice Warder Seely's clay figure evokes the *Last Song of the Plains*, a tribute to the power of the horse in Native cultures.

history, its landscape, its fantastic sunlight with ever-changing shadows, and the faces and character of my fellow New Mexicans."

RANDALL BLAZE

Working out of his studio in Cornelius, Oregon, Randall Blaze creates contemporary earthenware vessels with precious metal and stone inlays that pay homage to his ancestors. In his artistic journey, he integrates the visual elements of the Lakota Nation into the contemporary mainstream of the design world. "I search within myself to find guidance within the spirit of the morning star, the eye of the heart," he says.

Lakota Sioux artist Randall Blaze infuses his mixed-media earthenware-and-bronze vessels with poetry. Ancestral images inspire Randall's expressions of primal unity.

Opposite: For Randall Blaze, the spirit of the buffalo as a dream image or an earthenware symbol enables the union of humanity and cosmos.

A 1997 graduate of the University of Montana, Blaze draws inspiration from ancestral designs that address what he calls "the basic essence of our existence, our primal drive for unity within the orbit of the earth and the moon and stars."

Buffalo and lizards are two recurring themes in his work. He says, "I pass on the spirit of the buffalo as a dream image, the union of humanity and the cosmos. I pass on the spirit of the lizard to enrich the journey of others. I am guided within this spirit to sanctify happiness, fertility, and good fortune."

His vessels are as poignant and lyrical as his poetry.

MORNING STAR FOREVER

A butterfly touches the riverbank
and fades into a rainbow mist.

A woman rises there
cleansed by the water.

She chants a water song
and a wind song.

She is the only voice
until the rising of the sun.

Then all voices sing of the sun
and the rainbow on the riverbank.

A light breathes on her
and enters the sky in her head,

Leaving an amber glow persisting,
flowing for her vision.

She embraces the sun with love
and the sky with life.

She is called Morning Star
Forever

—Randall Blaze

SARAH PAUL BEGAY

Like many Native American artisans, Sarah Paul Begay learned weaving from her grandmother, Ella Greymountain, who made Begay card and spin wool in return for food. By the time she was seven, she had sold her first Navajo rug to the Indian Wells Trading Post for seven dollars.

Today, Begay is grateful for her grandmother's teachings. "I think she saw my determination to better myself," she said. After marriage and a decade of odd jobs, Begay returned to the loom. In 1986, she began selling her animated Hopi kachina rugs to the Heard Museum. A year later, this rug style became her trademark.

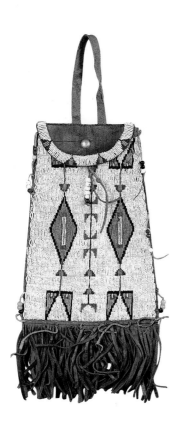

Working at her loom in Indian Wells, Arizona, Begay weds Two Grey Hills designs from the 1800s with yei-bi-chei dancers to add animation to her work.

"I always wanted to be different from all weavers. I wanted my own designs so my imagination could run wild. I never wanted to repeat the same old designs," Begay said. "I wanted my rugs to be on the walls and to be viewed as art."

RENA BEGAY

As a young girl growing up in Piñon, Arizona, Rena Begay learned every step of the weaving process from her aunt and mother at their looms. She sheared the sheep, carded the wool, and learned to spin, dye, and wash the wool. By age seventeen, she had completed her first rug, on her own, a Two Grey Hills design.

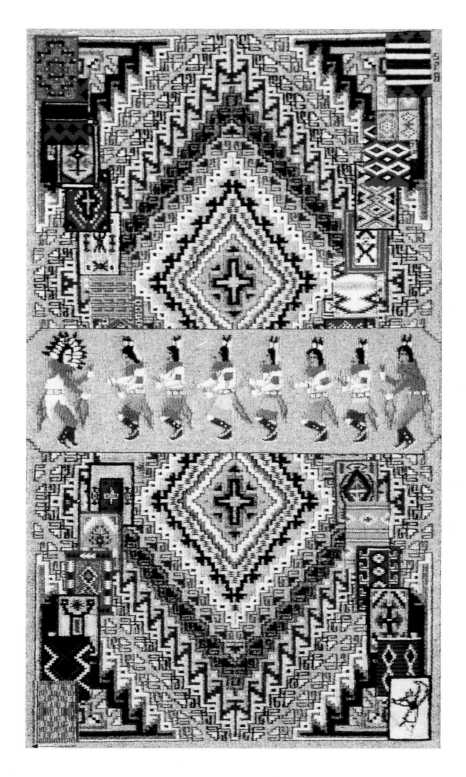

Navajo weaver Sarah Paul Begay crafted this brilliant masterpiece titled *The Navajo* in honor of her father, Raymond Paul. The rug features a Two Grey Hills background with animated yei-bi-chei dancers in the center. The rug was created in 1993 and hung in the National Cowboy Hall of Fame in 1997.

Opposite: An ornately beaded 1915 Lakota pouch expresses the geometric designs that are indicative of the Native American culture. This artifact was a gift to the National Cowboy Hall of Fame from Malcolm Doran Taylor and the Mark Devin Taylor Trust.

For five years, she shared the tools of a weaver with her aunt and mother until she received her own set of sacred tools when she was in her early twenties. To a Native American craftsman, receiving one's own set of tools is a significant rite of passage since tools are given only to those who show great promise.

Building on the Two Grey Hills tradition, she added her Chief's Blanket design in 1983 but began pushing for beautiful color and

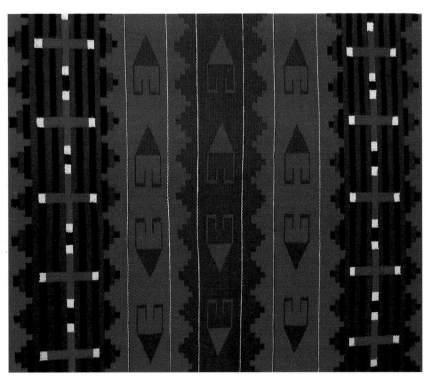

Piñon, Arizona, weaver Rena Begay marries traditional Chief's Blanket designs, such as crosses and stripes, with brilliant Ganado red coloring.

design variations within this style. Today her work features such traditional motifs as pueblo outlines, crosses, triangles, diamonds, and squares—often sparked with well-placed traceries of white. Her variations on traditional themes have become her trademark, along with the densely woven and balanced qualities of her rugs. Begay consistently wins top awards at arts and crafts shows in New Mexico, Arizona, and California.

THE HOPE SERIES

Four prominent Native American artists have directed their talents toward a pictorial blanket series produced by Pendleton Woolen Mills to benefit the American Indian College Fund. The

Lakota Sioux artist Arthur Amiotte created this striking *Day and Night Robe* for the American Indian College Fund. It is derived from traditional beaded strip blankets—red symbolizes sacred days and deep indigo the night.

artists are Tony Abeyta, a Navajo; Arthur Amiotte, a Lakota Sioux; George Hunt Jr., a Kwakiutl; and Wendy Ponca, an Osage.

The original blanket designs, produced in a limited edition of 1,200 for each blanket, commemorate tribes of the Northwest Coast, the Southwest, the Northern Plains, and the Osage People.

Abeyta's *Tree of Life* is inspired by old Navajo pictorial blankets and features twelve distinct colors in a design that includes an elaborate treelike cornstalk with birds. Corn, a staple of the Native American diet, symbolizes fertility and prosperity, and birds represent long life and robust health.

Abeyta, well known for his abstract depictions of American Indian deities, is from a large family of Navajo artisans. A Ford Foundation Scholar at Chicago's Art Institute, he studied fine arts in Europe and while in the Master's Studies Program at the Santa Fe Institute of Fine Art.

Amiotte's *Day and Night Robe* is a version of the traditional beaded Strip Blanket. The red (day) and blue (night) halves symbolize sacred days and nights. The blankets originally were made of bison hide, and the seam joining the two hides was concealed by a beaded strip. Amiotte's work is exhibited internationally, and he frequently serves as a consultant to museums and art institutes around the world.

Hunt's Chilkat-style blanket is titled *Tribute to My Grandmother Mary Ebbets Anislaga* and is reminiscent of carved cedar masks. As Tlingit legend relates, Anislaga was the living link between the ancient Tlingit culture and contemporary tribal weaving traditions. In ceremonies, the blanket is "danced," bringing to life the story of how Mankind was taught to weave by Raven, Lynx, Sea Monster, and Bear. When worn, these sacred images surround the wearer.

Hunt is also a renowned Northwest Coast wood-carver whose tribe originated on Vancouver Island. He learned his art at the

Taos artist William Acheff has earned a distinctive reputation for his use of Native American ceremonial objects that form the pivotal focal point of his paintings. In *Hopi Gods*, two kachina dolls flank a large vessel, and corn, the staff of Native American life, is positioned in the foreground.

knees of his grandfather and father, both respected carvers and tribal elders.

Ponca's *Wah-sha-she* was inspired by the broadcloth blankets worn by the Osage as they relinquished their buckskins more than a century ago. It is characterized by solid colors and bright borders. The Wah-sha-she were the first of the Plains Indians to have peaceful relations with the newly arrived European settlers. The hands represent that friendly contact; the dark green and gold symbolize the abundant, fruitful earth; and the ribbon work, with its stylized feathers and arrowheads, speaks of tribal strength.

Ponca began weaving, beading, and creating ribbon work and clothing design when she was six years old. She has won seven first-place awards at the Indian Market in Santa Fe, and her work is part of permanent museum collections throughout the nation.

WILLIAM ACHEFF

With an ethnic background that includes Georgian and Athabascan Indians and Russian, Scottish, and Dutch ancestors, William Acheff brings to his art a rich multicultural heritage. In 1973, he moved to Taos where Native Americans continue to provide him with a variety of inspiring subjects to paint, including pottery, blankets, drums, and other items indigenous to their life and culture. Acheff creates cultural commentaries, and he has long considered Native American pots as "old friends" for painting subjects, returning to them time and again for artistic inspiration. Native American weavings, beaded artifacts, and the photographs of Edward S. Curtis are other favorite

Nathan Youngblood's Santa Clara Pueblo pottery is a blend of earth, wind, and fire. This vessel reveals how Youngblood has carefully hand carved an intricate design using familiar Native American symbols.

subjects. His glistening oil portrayals of beadwork have given him a reputation for outstanding photo-realism.

He said, "I find artifacts and traditions of the past seem to hold more mystical and aesthetic value than those of contemporary times." In his still lifes, he combines a sensitivity for his subjects with his desire to paint the silence, the essence of the object. He often emulates the Dutch still life painters of the seventeenth and nineteenth centuries, among them the Harnett trompe l'oeil school. But always, Acheff is inspired by Native American themes.

NATHAN YOUNGBLOOD

In the tradition of his ancestors and to the delight of his grandmother teacher, Nathan Youngblood's Santa Clara Pueblo pottery is a blend of earth, wind, and fire. Wherever he goes, he carries in his heart the joy of making pottery—a gift from his ninety-three-year-old grandmother. "She is geared," he said, "to the happiness of life."

Youngblood's award-winning ceramic bowls and platters tell the story of his own life and his ancestors before him, of the New Mexico hills and streams, and of the golden deserts. His hands recount tales as they stretch and beat and shape the clay. His water jars and fruit bowls give themselves to the stories he perhaps no longer remembers. His plates are intricately and perfectly carved. They have been shown at the White House, the National Museum of American Art, and Gilcrease Museum.

"My work is on display in art galleries in Santa Fe and Scottsdale. And a plate, nowadays," he said with a grin, "can buy a good life for my family and me." His plates are collectors' items. Their soft whirled edges sing of old times and older traditions. They mirror his joy and that of his grandmother.

ZUNI FURNITURE ENTERPRISE

Entrepreneurship has long been a hallmark of the Zuni Pueblo, among the oldest (seven centuries) and largest (7,000 members) of Native American communities. Located thirty miles south of Gallup, New Mexico, Zuni was the site of the first fateful encounter between Coronado's expedition of 1540 and a Southwestern Native culture.

Throughout the long Spanish colonial period, which ended with Mexican independence in 1821, Pueblo craftsmen were trained in carpentry, blacksmithing, and building construction. But the Zuni

Young furniture craftsmen at Zuni Pueblo in western New Mexico incorporate carved and painted pottery designs, fetish figures, and textile patterns in their creations.

Furniture Enterprise, launched in 1991, marked the first time a south-western tribe had produced its own furniture based on tribal designs.

The furniture is reminiscent of prehistoric Zuni designs. Painted and carved representations of sacred animals and spiritual beings, called kachinas, decorate the basic pine furnishings. Pottery and weaving motifs also are used to grace folding screens, benches, chairs, and *trasteros*, or large upright cabinets.

The Zuni Pueblo also recently launched another venture—its own publishing company, Zuni Ashiwi Publishing—in an effort to publish books on all aspects of Zuni life—books that will help preserve the Zuni culture for future generations.

MIKE LARSEN

Mike Larsen, a Chickasaw, is known for his brilliantly colored portraits of shamans with exaggerated features. Larsen describes a shaman in the Native American culture as "one who reaches into other realms of existence to bring new meanings and answers to his people as they travel their journey in this life." In a similar analogy, Larsen parallels the ancient shaman's quest with that of the modern artist: to give to his audience an insight into what he perceives as the mysteries of the spirit.

Larsen studied at the University of Houston and then completed his education at the Art Students League of New York. It was later in his career that he defined his trademark of exaggerated hands. But to him, hands have a much deeper meaning. "Hands have the ability to generate, receive, store, and radiate all power," Larsen said. "A person's life and livelihood, the very essence of his being, cannot be hidden. His hands reflect all that he is."

Chickasaw artist Mike Larsen employs the pictorial technique of exaggerated human features, such as heads and hands, to invoke a shamanistic spirit and feeling of the mystical in his work.

Through distortion and exaggeration, he emphasizes this precious power shared by all mankind. His subjects' distorted hands invoke a sense of ancient man and woman, which Larsen believes adds a mystical feeling to his work.

A handsome leather hombre chair and companion ottoman were designed by the National Upholstering Company. Draped with an old Native American blanket and a traditional hemp rope, this duo would be a charming asset to any home.

NON-NATIVE DESIGNERS
NATIONAL UPHOLSTERING COMPANY
THE WESTERN COLLECTION

The Western Collection from the National Upholstering Company (NUC) was inspired by a battle scene painted on a 125-year-old buffalo hide by Plains Indians. The scene was so enchanting to NUC's third-generation president, Don Silva, that he commissioned a contemporary Native American artist to reinterpret those old scenes and designs.

He also wanted them painted on the wrong side of the leather so the furnishings looked rustic, "like they just came out of a bunkhouse." The resulting collection includes beautiful leathers, accented with leather laces and hand-stitched fringe. Nail heads, conchos, ledger drawings, and symbolic motifs familiar in the Native American culture are other design elements of this culturally inspired furniture.

Colorful native blankets or cowhide are used to upholster benches and sofas or double as accent pillows for these furnishings that truly reflect the Native spirit.

MARY COLTER
HARVEY HOUSE RAILROAD HOTELS

Before Native American design was widely recognized for its true genius, it was embraced and championed by architect Mary Colter (1869–1958). As a staff architect for the National Park Service and also for legendary hotelier Fred Harvey of the Santa Fe Railroad, Colter helped shape modern perceptions of Native American design. Her buildings have endured and are now recognized as masterpieces of southwestern architecture.

Mary Colter was trained in the Craftsman tradition near the turn of the century. At the San Francisco School of Design, she soaked up the Craftsman philosophy from such teachers as Bernard Maybeck and Arthur Mathews. Throughout her life, she had a natural affinity for arts and crafts, designing her own style of Mission furniture and learning metalwork and silversmithing. Her sensitivity to craftsmanship inevitably led to her passionate interest in Native American arts and crafts and architecture.

Among Colter's most remarkable buildings are the great Harvey House railroad hotels such as El Navajo in Gallup, New Mexico, and La Posada in Winslow, Arizona; the Fred Harvey shop interiors in Albuquerque and Santa Fe; and the National Park Service buildings at the Grand Canyon. Colter's designs for Hopi House, the Desert View Watchtower, the Lookout, and Hermit's Rest are all inspired by ancient Anasazi masonry and seem to emerge from the canyon walls. Colter constantly sought the insights of Native American artists and craftsmen, and Hopi workers were instrumental in the construction of the Grand Canyon structures. With Fred Harvey's patronage and vision, Mary Colter played a crucial role in exposing Native American arts and crafts to a national audience. Another example is seen in the Harvey Company's Indian shops, which she designed in an inspired blend of rustic and eclectic romanticism. The Indian Building next to the Alvarado Hotel in Albuquerque and Santa Fe's La Fonda

Adobe and log architecture combine dramatically in this corner Kiva fireplace setting.

Hotel were the showcases of Native American design talent for the better part of the twentieth century.

Perhaps Colter's greatest triumph was Gallup's El Navajo Hotel. In 1923, nearly 2,000 Native Americans attended the dedication of the El Navajo, including thirty medicine men who performed ritual prayers throughout the hotel to dispel evil spirits. It was a fitting tribute for Mary Colter's vision of Native American design. Largely

Architect Mary Colter was among the first designers to successfully employ Native American style in a large-scale commercial building. Her 1923 lobby for Gallup's El Navajo Hotel was commissioned by Fred Harvey, establishing a sophisticated standard.

demolished in 1957, the depot was dramatically rehabilitated by the community in 1994–95. The building's exterior design blended the typical apartment house, merging forms of Pueblo villages with modernist styling to produce a Pueblo Deco architectural landmark. Inside the building, authentic Navajo sandpaintings on the walls accented the interiors filled with Mission and wicker furniture, producing one of the first large-scale examples of Native American-influenced interior design.

Master stonemason Michael Lyn Stearns's company, Flowing Waters of Stone, produced brilliant Anasazi-style walls for Santa Fe's Inn of the Anasazi.

Opposite: New West furniture company of Cody, Wyoming, offers a "Thunderbird" credenza accented with cut-steel arrow drawer pulls and leather top.

MICHAEL LYN STEARNS
FLOWING WATERS OF STONE

Michael Lyn Stearns was born in the heart of prehistoric Pueblo country in Casa Grande, Arizona. As a fourth-generation stonemason, Michael was destined to learn about the Southwest's intricate Anasazi stonework.

After a trip to Chaco Canyon in the spring of 1985, Michael's life was transformed. In his words, "I was not prepared for the inspiration and beauty of the [Anasazi] stonework that literally consumed my vision as a stonemason. The architectural genius that had passed from generation to generation sent chills all over my body. New creative vision rushed through me!"

Stearns founded his masonry company, Flowing Waters of Stone, in Santa Fe, where he and his team of masons have perfected the fine art of Anasazi masonry on display in many of the city's finest homes and public spaces. Water has always been cherished in the Anasazi homeland and inspires the name and motto of Stearns's company. "Waterfalls create soothing and magical sounds and a feeling of serenity. Flowing Waters of Stone can bring this harmony into your space."

J. MIKE PATRICK
NEW WEST DESIGNS

No part of the United States has ever captured the hearts and minds of the American people as much as the West. To J. Mike Patrick and his wife, Virginia, the West has defined for many Americans what they dream to be the national character.

The Patricks have been leaders in the renaissance of western-inspired design, creating furnishings that reflect cowboy and Indian themes. Originally inspired by the work of Thomas Molesworth, they now push their imagination well beyond it.

From drum tables and leather drapes to chandeliers and furniture, their Native-inspired New West collection features all the familiar motifs—buffalo, bears, Indians on horseback, chiefs in war bonnets, ledger drawings, and ancient weavings.

Mike Patrick said, "These are our interpretation of Native American designs. We are scrupulous about never directly copying any work of Native American art. We love the imagery and find it an especially compelling source of graphics for our decorative art."

JOHN BAUER

John Bauer began making furniture as sculpture. A geology graduate of Vanderbilt University, Bauer now works from his studio in Santa Fe. His design goal is "to create a visual flow and rhythm creating unity of form shaped by function. Similarities to traditional designs occur from function, rather than an influence from historic styles."

Bauer is noted for his chair series based on old photographs of Apache scouts, Hopi sisters, Navajos, and the great Comanche chief Quanah Parker. But he also draws on the Mimbres and Anasazi cultures. Lizards, rattlesnakes, rabbits, and birds often embellish his work.

Wood is his medium of choice. "I was first attracted to it because of its availability, naturalness and workability with simple tools.

Through the years I have learned its strengths, beauties, and limitations," Bauer said. Walnut, cherry, Honduras mahogany, and madrona are sometimes accented with glass and marble.

A highboy from New West Designs of Cody boasts a painted Plains Indian scene set within a wormwood and burl frame.

Opposite: Santa Fe Craftsman John Bauer incorporates carvings of Comanche heroes Chief Quanah Parker on the right and Chief Tosh-a-wah on the left of his walnut "Comanche" chair. The back inlay design is an abstracted buffalo hide, a source of the Plains lifestyle.

Bauer said, "I like forms that lead the eye all about a piece. I use animals, figures, and other imagery to stimulate feelings and memories. The curves and polished surfaces of my work invite the hand to touch."

JEREMY MORELLI

Jeremy Morelli's doors and furniture echo the ancient traditions and textiles of the Anasazi, Mayans, and Spanish Moors with new designs that incorporate superb carving, hand-hewn texturing, and the use of native colors and aged finishes.

Flowers and birds from the jungles of Aztec Mexico or the forests of the Pacific Northwest are intricately carved into wood. An elaborate chief's headdress inspires a mirror frame or a bed's headboard. Furnishings hand carved by the late Russian-born artist

A dining ensemble by West by Southwest of Farmington, New Mexico, incorporates Navajo yei figures with stylized cornstalk designs.

Opposite: Santa Fe master craftsman Jeremy Morelli developed the "Anasazi" series of remarkable doorways inspired by the ancient Anasazi tradition of covering doorways with beautiful weavings.

Nicolai Fechin inspire Morelli's doors, chairs, and credenzas—furnishings that invite one to feel the depth of texture and to gaze at the rich mirrorlike patinas.

From their Santa Fe studio, Morelli and his team of craftsmen bring these wondrous design ideas to life in the form of cultural masterpieces. He said, "What I'm trying to establish in my studio is something like the old guilds of Europe. And as the visionary, I'm constantly looking for new design approaches."

The result is furniture that expresses the romance of the past and the eclectic theme of contemporary life, created with today's most progressive technology.

GUYLYN DURHAM
WEST BY SOUTHWEST

Growing up in New Mexico gave Guylyn Durham a deep appreciation of Native American art. She studied under a number of southwestern artists and developed her own distinctive vocabulary of design. Inspired by the region's petroglyphs, pottery, rugs, and jewelry, she creates intriguing steel sculptures and furnishings that reflect upon and illuminate past traditions.

In 1990, she established West by Southwest as a cottage industry in northwest New Mexico and quickly achieved international acclaim for her work. She is now represented in galleries, museums, and national monuments across the United States.

She calls the unique quality of her work "originality through isolation" and frequently turns to the ancient Native artists for

A cut-steel-and-glass sconce by New West Designs invokes Native American style with minimalist and modern sensibility.

Opposite: Aspen Mountain is a dramatic backdrop for a spectacular Native American-inspired interior by Cassandra Lohr.

inspiration. "I hold these artists in highest esteem for their great insight into style," she said, "which often projects a contemporary feeling when adapted to steel. As a voyager through this timeless land, I aspire to interpret and extend the art forms rooted in our southwest American heritage."

CASSANDRA LOHR
OLD WEST COLLECTION

Cassandra Lohr created an Aspen, Colorado, company based on the magic and romance of the Old West. She offers traditional furnishings, artifacts, and accessories handcrafted by numerous artisans, many whose heritage is Native American. Hers is a collaborative, cross-cultural approach to this design style.

She achieved national notice when, in August 1994, a tipi she designed for a client's Aspen retreat was featured on the cover of *Architectural Digest*. It featured the inside, which included a burled-wood bed, tables with inlaid-tile designs derived from quilts, and antler lamps. Navajo rugs, blankets, sheets, and pillowcases, which found their birthright in ancient ledger drawings, completed the look.

Inspired and enchanted by the Southwest's history, Lohr said, "The making of these objects is almost a lost art today. Manufacturers cannot create the beauty and feel of handmade. Factories cannot reproduce the colors from the earth and sky that saturate western sunsets and canyon lands. Nor can they replicate the smell of burnished leather of a well-worn saddle, or the natural, spontaneous weave of geometric designs on native pottery."

Arizona artist Ray Swanson has devoted his career to painting the people of the reservations, especially the Navajo. In *Newest to the Flock*, a young Indian maiden gets acquainted with a special friend—a new baby lamb. Swanson says, "The goats and sheep have been an integral part of the lives of the Navajo people since their introduction to the reservation. These animals have provided for many of their daily needs, from mutton to eat and wool for weaving traditional rugs."

RAY SWANSON

For more than three decades, Ray Swanson has been chronicling life on the Navajo Reservation through oil paintings. For Swanson, it all started with a Fourth of July powwow in the early 1960s.

He was instantly fascinated with the vital colors of Navajo life—the royal purples and greens of the Navajo dress, the velvet blouses, the silver and turquoise, the browned faces, the dark eyes and hair, and the red buttes against all that blue sky punctuated with clouds. His paintings reflect the artistic balance he strives to achieve—a full and expressive life on the countenance of the elders; expectancy and readiness on the face of a child.

"I felt an urgency to capture the life and times of the Navajo before too many changes took place," Swanson said. "And I didn't know when I started that I would be sketching history." Since then, his Native American friends have become more than compadres, more than family. They are his soul, and it shows in his work.

THE ELIZABETH DREY COLLECTION

Elizabeth Drey traveled all over the world before she moved to Santa Fe in 1991. The impetus for the move was a desire to open a store where she could sell artifacts from her many travels. Santa Fe, with its intriguing blend of cultures, beckoned.

But it wasn't long before her background as a designer of stores, interiors, and furniture came into play. The romantic mix of the Spanish, Anglo, and Mexican cultures inspired her to create a new line of furnishings.

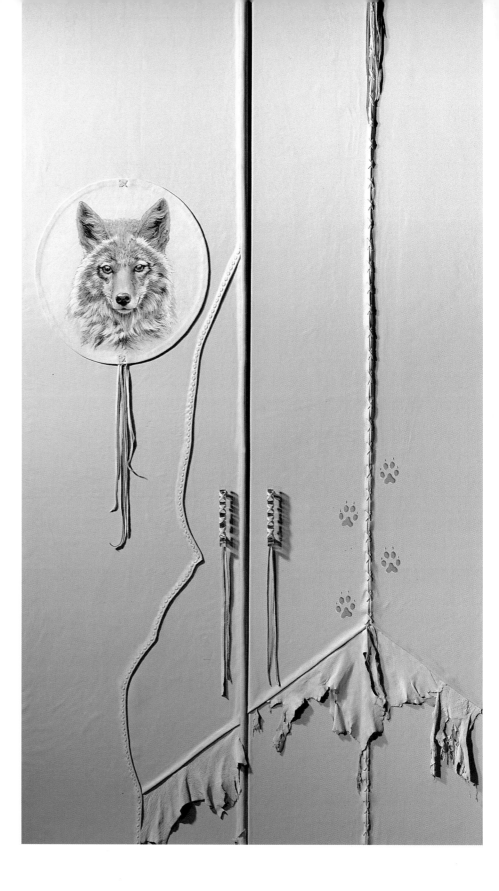

These striking coyote panels are the creation of Elizabeth Drey.

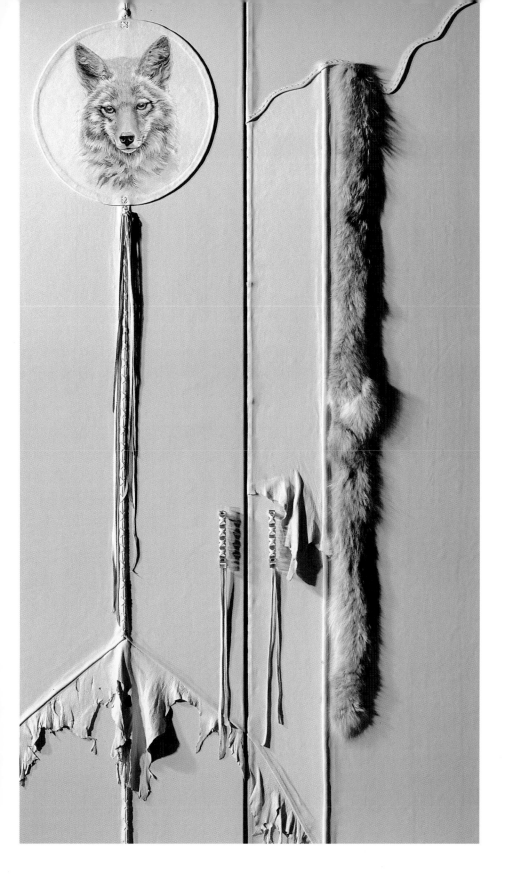

Her first piece was a sofa. "I had scheduled the opening of my store and didn't have much to show," she recalled. "So I bought this

Santa Fe designer Elizabeth Drey combines numerous Native American apparel motifs to create a sumptuous buckskin throne.

Opposite: A scorpion design derived from ancient Mimbres pottery of southwestern New Mexico is the centerpiece of a coffee table by Santa Fe's Gunther Worrlein.

expensive sofa in Albuquerque, and we tore it up for five days and managed to cover it in suede." It was a big hit and an auspicious beginning for the Elizabeth Drey Collection.

Now custom-leather easy chairs, ottomans, and, of course, sofas feature luxurious backdrops for designs inspired by Navajo rug patterns, Zuni rainbird motifs, and Pueblo designs. Horses are a new motif in the collection. Fringe, nail heads, and prayer feathers are finishing touches.

Not content to just design furniture, Drey and her Navajo production staff also create throw pillows and western-style leather jackets.

GUNTHER WORRLEIN
WORRLEIN STUDIOS

An observer of the Mimbres culture of southwestern New Mexico once remarked in the *Illustrated London News*, "What impresses us most is the disparity between the highly developed sense of design possessed by the Mimbres craftsmen and their primitive mode of life."

It was the precise perfection of the Mimbres designs that drove Gunther Worrlein to create furniture adorned with the elegant and ethereal animal imagery that symbolizes the Mimbres motifs. "It's impossible not to be attracted by their designs—they're so perfect," he said.

In chairs and credenzas, chests and armoires, Worrlein said, "I try to elaborate and put my own expression on the traditional styles. Even the Egyptians built upon older traditions. I really appreciate some of the new directions that New Mexico furniture is taking. My work is built upon the traditional, but it has my own personality, which likes the grand gesture."

Worrlein brings to his designs the creative expression he acquired while training in Italy as well as the Chippendale influences he found while living in New Orleans. His wife, Joan, is part of the team, finishing the pieces and giving him design advice.

RICHARD GREEVES

Richard Greeves often says his destiny as an artist was shaped by a trip he took when he was fifteen years old. A native of St. Louis, Missouri, he traveled to Fort Washakie on the Wind River Reservation in Wyoming. It was a brief respite from school, but the journey and his time spent with an Indian family left an indelible impression on him.

Greeves returned home to finish school, but he knew that the Wind River Reservation had stolen his heart. Several years later he returned there, and for more than three decades, he has made his home on the reservation among the North American Plains Indians.

In that time, Greeves has forged out of the whole cloth of Native America a unique lifestyle centered around his artistic capabilities as an award-winning sculptor. He portrays the character and spiritual essence of the people and animals of his chosen homeland. "There is a magic, a mysticism for me here that I really can't explain. I just feel it," he said. "In my work, I'm just trying in my meager way to bridge this civilization with ones that come after us."

SHIRLEY THOMSON-SMITH

Elegant and sophisticated are often the words used to describe the sleek sculpture of Shirley Thomson-Smith, a native of St. Louis, Missouri, who has lived most of her life in Oklahoma City, Oklahoma. She is quick to say, however, that it was a move to Durango,

Colorado, that changed her life and forged the direction of her art. While living there, she met many Navajo women united by gender and the fact that they had dominant husbands. Thomson-Smith developed an admiration for the resilience and silent strength they displayed.

Sculptor Shirley Thomson-Smith has long been influenced by Native American women, and this bronze, titled *Hopi Maiden*, reflects that interest. Smith says, "I've always admired Mexican, African, and Indian art. My figures are a synthesis of all these, particularly the strength and sturdiness inherent in Mexican and Native American women."

Opposite: Richard V. Greeves, a sculptor who makes his home on the Wind River Reservation in Wyoming, is known for his unique bronze portrayals of Native American figures and legends. Of this work, titled *Can You See?*, Greeves says, "It sounds so simple, but think of all the many ways we are confronted with that question—joyfully, inquisitively, angrily, and as a matter of fact. All of these thoughts were finding their way through my mind as I worked creating this sculpture. A big thought, hidden under the simple action of the two hunters trying to see."

Over time, that admiration blossomed into deep respect and affection. "The memories of those years have provided a wealth of feelings and emotions," she said. "I was fascinated by them. Their message was a nonverbal transmission of thought, feeling, and strength."

Thomson-Smith has always admired Mexican, African, and Indian art. "My figures are a synthesis of all these, particularly the strength and sturdiness inherent in Mexican and Native American women," she said. The result is Native-inspired sculpture that is strong and powerful. She breathes life into her figures and, with simplicity, bares their souls.

This stunning cabinet is the work of Santa Fe artist Ray Fisher.

Opposite: Cody master craftsman Lester Santos of Santos Furniture produces a ledger club chair with painted Sioux designs.

LESTER SANTOS
SANTOS FURNITURE

Lester Santos's handcrafted furniture combines the earthy, rustic simplicity of western design with Native American motifs, expressed in sophisticated and intricate carving. Santos often uses burled wood as the basis for his designs. With its strange shapes that are sometimes whimsical, sometimes bizarre, burled wood provides an unusual visual and textural contrast to his soft-to-the-touch leathers, suedes, and hides.

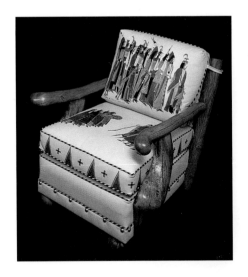

Twig and root furniture is often considered as classic folk art, but with Santos's addition of Native American motifs painted on leather, these furnishings are elevated to fine art. Historic ledger drawings, ceremonial scenes, and motifs drawn from nature, the cosmos, and geometric symbols grace his designs.

Santos and his talented team of craftsmen are continuing a Wyoming tradition by carefully reproducing the wood and leather furniture first made in the 1930s in Cody by Thomas Molesworth.

RAY FISHER
SANTA FE, NEW MEXICO

When Ray Fisher and his wife Alice left New Jersey more than a decade ago and headed for Santa Fe, they had no idea how much they would be influenced by the southwestern landscape and its rich multicultural environment. Yet they were looking for fresh visions and new challenges, and the Southwest yielded an unexpected bounty for them. Ray was trained at the Newark School of Fine and Industrial

Santa Fe artist Ray Fisher's
Pueblo deco armoire is
influenced by ornamentation
on a train depot.

Arts and has always expressed a freewheeling imagination in his work. His restless curiosity only serves to enhance his visions.

The hallmarks of his furniture designs and light fixtures are a blend of the past with futuristic materials. Much of his recent work takes its inspiration from the Art Deco period, yet the southwestern Native American themes are always apparent, albeit in subtle ways.

He adapts details from Pueblo Deco buildings, especially the Southern Pacific Train Station in Casa Grande, Arizona. Particularly striking is a parapet design on a Southwestern Deco armoire. Such materials as Corian, usually more at home in kitchens, find their way into his striking collection of ethereally translucent light fixtures. Never content with his latest achievements, Fisher is always looking for a new horizon to conquer. Currently, he's considering inspirations from the 1950s—all with a southwestern, Native American touch.

BILL WORRELL

A six-day odyssey in 1979 down the last sixty-six miles of the Lower Pecos River marked the genesis of Bill Worrell's artistic emphasis. It was here that Worrell personally observed pictographic vestiges of an ancient American culture of primitive people who occupied rock shelters and began painting around 3500–3000 B.C., mysteriously vanishing around A.D. 1000.

These pictographic images, seemingly an amalgamation of animal and human characteristics, embellish the shelters in stunning and mystical silence. They are believed to be the artwork of shamans,

L. D. Burke III, a Santa Fe artisan who converted an old church for his studio, created this distressed-wood mirror frame for the Saudi Prince Bandar. The frame features Indian medicine bags, buffalo-nickel accents, and one of Burke's trademark thought-provoking mottoes. This one, "If you love beautiful things, love yourself."

Opposite: Bill Worrell's shaman sculpture is titled *From the Soul of Women*. The work is representative of his highly stylized, almost mystical Native American bronze sculptures.

who held positions of ultimate respect and cultural significance and acted as mediators between the people and the spirits of nature. They sought to establish harmony with nature's rhythms by asking restitution for use of the earth's life-sustaining bounties—a quest for harmony with the universe.

For Worrell, this discovery was powerful—an experience that would forever change the direction and style of his work. Now working out of his home and studio on the banks of the Llano River near the small town of Art in the Texas Hill Country, he maintains that, aesthetically, his shaman sculptures and paintings are interpretations of the ancient pictographs rather than a documentation of their historical value.

Worrell said, "My work, my paintings, sculptures, and jewelry are about the spirit of man, the spirit of woman. It is about eternity, about human destiny. It is about restitution, wonderings, wanderings, and longings. It is about fulfillment, expectations, and primitive minds. It is about religion and thought, about matter and consciousness. It is about human soul and about how these things, and other things, have been made manifest through the minds and hands and the personalities and essences of the ancient shamans of the Lower Pecos and its confluence with the Rio Grande."

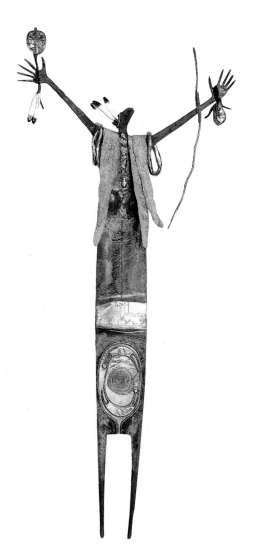

From the soul of woman
Comes my soul.
From her mind
Came my learning,
My reason,
And my dreams.
—Bill Worrell

No art remains static and survives. Even though traditions may temporarily satisfy a sense of unity, innovations seek to overwhelm them, making Native American works one of the most active, interesting fields of art today.
— Barton Wright
Native American art authority

RICK BARTHOLOMEW
NATIVE LINES

As a professor of design, housing, and merchandising at Oklahoma State University in Stillwater, Rick Bartholomew's creative designs reflect his long-standing interest in Native American, southwestern, and Art Deco design styles, as well as the writings and teachings of Frank Lloyd Wright.

The interest has culminated in a line of furnishings called Native Lines, that draws its inspiration from the graphic symbols of the Five Civilized Tribes of the Native American culture— Cherokee, Chickasaw, Choctaw, Creek, and Seminole. The furnishings, for home and office, are produced in cooperation with the Oklahoma Fixture Company in Tulsa. Native Lines was unveiled in an exhibition in June 1998 at the Five Civilized Tribes Museum in Muskogee, Oklahoma.

Every piece in the collection was designed to illustrate the diversity and richness of each tribe's history and culture. The designs and colors used in the execution of the furniture summon forth images of these tribes' daily and ceremonial life. The furniture shows the variety, depth, and skill of their arts and crafts, and through these pieces, viewers gain a better understanding of the day-to-day activities of these remarkable peoples.

In the Cherokee-inspired pieces, the geometric twill-plaited pattern is reminiscent of basket weaving, and the insets of brown distressed leathers signify the use of hides and leathers as a daily staple commodity. The realistic side is called forth by the open-slat design

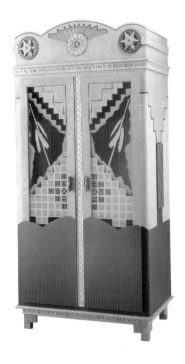

Oklahoman Rick Bartholomew drew on his fascination with Native American heritage to design this multipurpose curio cabinet, or memory chest, featuring motifs indigenous to the Seminole culture. The striking blend of tricolored woods and etched glass make this a cabinet that could go well in any Native American theme setting.

Opposite: Kathy Whiteman Elkwoman pays homage to the sacred and magical horse in her flowing sculpture.

Sleek bronze contemporary Native American figures by Allan Houser, a mother and child perhaps, stand as silent sentinels in this garden in the Southwest. Haunting yet poignant, these stylized "people" add artistic drama to the landscape.

Opposite: John B. Mortensen, a Wyoming artist and sculptor, is known for his unusual furnishings that blend the roughness of hand-hewn logs with his artistry in bronze. In this table, chair, and lamp, bronze buffalo figures and sturdy nail heads are used to embellish the Native American-style furnishings.

representing the feathery plumes worn by chieftains. The stair-stepped lines illustrate the "stairway to heaven" designs found in many craft items, such as baskets, blankets, and ceremonial dress.

The Chickasaw-inspired wardrobe cabinet illustrates the inspiring resolve of a nation's search for a homeland. The ancestral tale of the "sacred pole," recalling the Chickasaw's migration from the West to the southeastern United States, is clearly illustrated in this piece. According to legend, leaders placed a staff in the ground each night during their journey and in the morning, traveled in the direction the pole was leaning.

Renowned as the Chickasaw craftsmen are for their beadwork, the intricately carved feather and star medallions and banding are a symbolic tribute to their artistry. Also incorporated into the designs is their belief that they live in a circle, whereby the sun represents the power of life and death.

The Creek-inspired pieces symbolize the abstract geometric shapes used to adorn personal items, such as garments, headgear, and jewelry as well as domestic ones like pottery and baskets. Their use, in the form of Vs, Ws, diamonds, and triangles, is abundant.

The Seminole culture is known for metal jewelry adornment, especially the silver crescent-shaped gorgets, symbolizing a badge of rank among the Europeans. Decorative drawer and door pulls depict this cultural artistry and level of importance.

Bartholomew says the research for these furnishings was a quest to "visually document the graphic-design motifs that depict the various cultural and historical art forms and incorporate these graphic

illustrations into interior furnishings as a way to preserve an important part of our nation's heritage." This endeavor is in response to the
resurgence of a growing public awareness of Native American pride
and the importance of its people. Native Lines is truly an expression
of inspired American Indian symbolism.

RESOURCE GUIDE

American Indian College Fund
P.O. Box 397
Camden, NC 27921
1-800-987-FUND
Marketing unique Pendleton blankets designed by Native American artists

Rick L. Bartholomew, A.S.I.D., MS
Assistant Professor of
  Interior Design
Department of Design,
  Housing, and Merchandising
441 College of Human
  Environmental Sciences
Oklahoma State University
Stillwater, OK 74078
(405) 744-5035

John L. Bauer
25 Camino Oriente
Santa Fe, NM 87505
(505) 982-4399
Handcrafted and carved furniture featuring Native American and inlaid figures

Rena Begay
P.O. Box 69
Piñon, AZ 86510
(602) 725-3225
Prize-winning handcrafted Navajo tapestries

Sarah Paul Begay
P.O. Box 3037
Indian Wells, AZ 86031
Exceptional Navajo weavings

Randall Blaze
3975 N.W. Susbauer Road
Cornelius, OR 97113
Contemporary Lakota/Oglala ceramic art

Elizabeth Drey Collection
214 W. San Francisco Street
  Suite 306
Santa Fe, NM 87505
(505) 992-8708
Luxury fringed-leather furniture and accessories

James Ferrara
3310 Wallingford Ave. North
Seattle, WA 98103
Bannock/Shoshone craftsman of Plains and southwestern cultures handcrafted furniture

Ray Fisher
3 Amistad Place
Santa Fe, NM 87505
(505) 466-8949

Inn of the Anasazi
113 Washington Avenue
Santa Fe, NM 87501
(505) 988-3030
Luxury hotel appointed in the spirit of the ancient Anasazi

Cassandra Lohr Design International
P.O. Box 4611
Aspen, CO 81612
(303) 377-7121
Fine interior design and the creator of the Old West Collection of handcrafted Native American furniture and accessories

**Ron McGee
Wild West Furniture**
P.O. Box 3010
Apache Junction, AZ 85717
(602) 921-9808
Plains culture-inspired furniture

Jeremy Morrelli
131 Nusbaum
Santa Fe, NM 87501
(505) 984-1587
Superb carved furniture featuring Anasazi, Navajo, and Aztec designs

John B. Mortensen Studios
P.O. Box 746
Wilson, WY 83014
(307) 733-1519

National Upholstering Company
4000 Adeline Street
Oakland, CA 94608
(510) 653-8915
Western collection of sofas
and club chairs upholstered in
leather, native blankets, and
other western textiles

New West
2811 Big Horn Avenue
Cody, WY 82414
Molesworth and Plains
culture-influenced furniture
and accessories

Oklahoma Fixture Company
2900 East Apache Street
Tulsa, OK 74110
(918) 836-3794, Ext. 313
or 309 or 1-800-517-8419

Oklahoma Indian Art Gallery
Doris Littrell, Owner
2335 S.W. 44th Street
Oklahoma City, OK 73119
(405) 685-6162

Lester Santos
Santos Furniture
2202 Public Street
Cody, WY 82414
(307) 587-6543
Molesworth-inspired furniture
featuring fine western leathers
and painted Native American
designs

Alice Warder Seeley
P.O. Box 166
Hondo, NM 88336
Unique handcrafted and
painted accessory boxes

Stage West
P.O. Box 3100
Cody, WY 82414
(307) 527-6620
Buckskin upholstered cedar
chests inspired by the western
frontier

Michael Lyn Stearns
Flowing Waters of Stone
P.O. Box 8932
Santa Fe, NM 87501
(505) 988-5401
Intricate stone masonry in the
Anasazi tradition

Taos Drum Company, Inc.
P.O. Box 1916
Taos, NM 87571
1-800-424-DRUM
Marketing authentic Taos
drums, tipis, and other Native
American accessories

Ray Tracey
2100 A. Aztec
Albuquerque, NM 87107
(505) 883-8868

West by Southwest
2800 Inland Street
Farmington, NM 87401
Polished-metal furniture with
cutout shapes evoking
southwest petroglyphs—
Navajo and Pueblo designs

Western Canvas Supply and Repair
P.O. Box 1382
Cody, WY 82414
(307) 587-6707
Plain and painted tipis in the
Plains cultural tradition

Gunther Worrlein
Worrlein Studios
11 La Junta Road
Lamy, NM 87540
Furniture inspired by Mimbres
designs

Zuni Furniture Enterprise
P.O. Box 339
Zuni, NM 87327
(505) 782-5855
Handcrafted pine furniture
featuring Pueblo of Zuni
painted designs and fetish
symbols

PHOTOGRAPHIC CREDITS

Pages 2, 3, 6, 8, 14, 15, 18, 20, 24, 27, 53, 56, 57, 64, 65, 107, and 136 by Elmo Baca; Pages 70B and 71T courtesy Elmo Baca; Pages 10, 11, 49, and front cover by John Rozum; Half-title page and pages 52, 55, 58, and 76T by Lisa Wallace, Light Language Studio, courtesy Gallup Inter-tribal Indian Ceremonial; Page 5 courtesy Irving Toddy; Pages 16, 69, 70T, and 103 courtesy American Indian College Fund; Page 19 courtesy Gallup Inter-tribal Indian Ceremonial Association; Pages 22, 46, and 121 courtesy Cassandra Lohr; Pages 23, 76B, and 113 courtesy the Museum of New Mexico Photo Archives; Page 25 courtesy the Panhandle Plains Museum; Pages 28 and 59 courtesy Inn of the Anasazi; Page 48 courtesy Ron McGee; Pages 62, 63, and 139 courtesy John Mortensen; Page 71B courtesy Ramona Sakiestewa; Pages 73 and 101 courtesy Rena Begay; Pages 86, 90, and 134 courtesy L. D. Burke; Pages 87, 117, and 120 courtesy New West Furniture; Pages 94 and 95 courtesy James Ferrara; Pages 96 and 97 courtesy Alice Warder Seeley; Pages 98 and 99 courtesy Randall Blaze; Page 110 courtesy National Upholstery Company; Page 114 courtesy Flowing Waters of Stone; Page 116 courtesy John Bauer; Page 118 courtesy Guylyn Durham; Page 119 by Robert Reck, courtesy Jeremy Morelli; Pages 124, 125, and 126 courtesy Elizabeth Drey Collection; Page 127 courtesy Worrlein Studios; Pages 130 and 132 courtesy Ray Fisher; Page 131 courtesy Lester Santos; Page 135 courtesy Bill Worrell; Pages 17 and 75 courtesy the Museum Store at the National Cowboy Hall of Fame and Western Heritage Center, Oklahoma City, Oklahoma; Pages 17, 29, 84, and 100 courtesy the National Cowboy Hall of Fame and Western Heritage Center; Pages 66, 67, and 68 courtesy the John Wayne Collection at the National Cowboy Hall of Fame and Western Heritage Center; Page 74 courtesy the exhibit *Beyond Tradition* hosted by the National Cowboy Hall of Fame and Western Heritage Center; Pages 34, 35, 37, 38, 39, and 81 courtesy the Arthur and Shifra Silberman Collection at the National Cowboy Hall of Fame and Western Heritage Center; Page 41 courtesy the Taos Collection at the National Cowboy Hall of Fame and Western Heritage Collection; Page 25 courtesy the Panhandle Museum and Heritage Center, Canyon, Texas; Page 30 courtesy the Gilcrease Museum, Tulsa, Oklahoma; Page 32 courtesy a private collector; Page 43 courtesy Joan Frederick; Pages 42 and 122 courtesy Ray Swanson; Pages 51, 82, and 91 courtesy Alpine Log Homes, Victor, Montana; Page 54 by and copyright by Jerry Jacka; Page 77 courtesy Ray Tracey; Pages 88 and 89 courtesy Custom Log Homes, Inc., Stevensville, Montana; Page 92 courtesy Virginia Stroud and the Oklahoma Indian Art Gallery, Oklahoma City, Oklahoma; Page 105 courtesy William Acheff; Page 106 courtesy Nathan Youngblood; Page 109 courtesy Mike Larsen; Page 128 courtesy Richard V. Greeves; Page 129 by Ed Muno, courtesy Shirley-Thomson Smith; Page 137 courtesy Rick Bartholomew and the Oklahoma Fixture Company; Page 138 courtesy a private collector.

Architect John Midyette III of Santa Fe, New Mexico, designed this true adobe house in Santa Fe to take advantage of the phenomenal views of the Sangre de Cristo Mountains. Most of the interior walls curve to give a softness to the interior. The dining-room archway is faced with native stone.

Julia A. Redwine, of Studio One Design Incorporated in Lake Forest, Illinois, designed the interiors to be "warm and comfortable and capture all the views of the exterior." All of the logs were handpicked by the client, and many of the hand-hewn logs are of antique vintage.